THE GOOD EARTH

Pearl S. Buck

SPARK PUBLISHING

Spark Publishing
A Division of Barnes & Noble
120 Fifth Avenue
New York, NY 10011
www.sparknotes.com

ISBN-13: 978-1-4114-0733-6
ISBN-10: 1-4114-0733-4

Please submit changes or report errors to www.sparknotes.com/errors.

Printed in the United States.

10 9 8 7 6 5 4 3 2 1

Contents

Context

Pearl S. Buck was born in 1892 in Hillsboro, West Virginia, to Absalom and Carie Sydenstricker, two Christian missionaries. When Buck was three months old, her parents took her with them on a mission to China, where they spent most of the next forty years. Buck grew up playing with Chinese children, who referred to her as a "foreign devil." Although contempt of the Chinese was common among the families of Western Christian missionaries, Buck never developed that sense of superiority. Since Buck grew up in China, she was able to objectively recognize the absurdities of missionary work. Buck's objectivity is evident in her portrayal of Western missionaries in *The Good Earth*.

Buck returned to the United States to attend Randolph-Macon Woman's College in Lynchburg, Virginia, where she did well academically and achieved some measure of popularity. However, the country of her birth was largely unfamiliar to her, and she felt like a foreigner. After graduating, she returned to China to take care of her ailing mother. In 1917, she married John Lossing Buck, an agricultural economist and graduate of Cornell. Her first and only biological child, Carol, was born in 1921. Due to a uterine tumor discovered during the delivery, Buck had to undergo a hysterectomy. Soon after, Buck discovered that her daughter was severely retarded. Almost at the same time, Buck's mother died after a long illness. These misfortunes placed a great deal of strain on Buck's marriage. She divorced her husband in 1935 and married a man named Richard J. Walsh later the same year.

In 1931, Buck published *The Good Earth*, her second and best-known book. The novel, a complex moral parable that draws heavily on Buck's firsthand knowledge of Chinese culture, quickly gained an international reputation and won the Pulitzer Prize in 1932. Over the next few years, Buck wrote two sequels, *Sons* and *A House Divided*, but neither was as popular as *The Good Earth*. Buck also wrote biographies of her parents. Buck was awarded the Nobel Prize for literature in 1938, mainly in recognition of these biographies and *The Good Earth*.

Throughout her life, Buck devoted herself to humanitarian causes. She fought constantly on behalf of women's rights. With her husband, Richard Walsh, she founded an adoption agency for children of mixed Asian and American parentage. These children were often outcasts in Asian countries because of their mixed blood and because they were often the out-of-wedlock offspring of American servicemen. Buck also took an active interest in issues as diverse as the lives of immigrants in New York City and the independence movement in India. In addition to these various causes, she was a staunch supporter of free speech and civil liberties. Buck died in 1973 after a long and active life as an activist, a humanitarian, and a writer.

PLOT OVERVIEW

WANG LUNG IS A POOR YOUNG FARMER in rural, turn-of-the-century China. During the time in which the novel takes place, Chinese society is showing signs of modernization while remaining deeply connected to ancient traditions and customs. When Wang Lung reaches a marriageable age, his father approaches the powerful local Hwang family to ask if they have a spare slave who could marry his son. The Hwangs agree to sell Wang a 20-year-old slave named O-lan, who becomes his wife. O-lan and Wang Lung are pleased with each other, although they exchange few words and although Wang is initially disappointed that O-lan does not have bound feet.

Together, Wang Lung and O-lan cultivate a bountiful and profitable harvest from their land. O-lan becomes pregnant, and Wang Lung is overjoyed when O-lan's first child is a son. Meanwhile, the powerful Hwang family lives decadently—the husband is obsessed with women, and the wife is an opium addict. Because of their costly habits, the Hwangs fall on hard times, and Wang Lung is able to purchase a piece of their fertile rice land. He enjoys another profitable harvest, and O-lan gives birth to another son. Wang Lung's new wealth catches the attention of his greedy, lazy uncle. Custom dictates that Wang Lung must show the utmost respect to members of the older generation, especially relatives, so he is forced to loan his uncle money despite knowing that the money will be wasted on drinking and gambling. The Hwang family's finances continue to falter, and the Hwangs sell another tract of land to Wang Lung.

After O-lan gives birth to a daughter, a terrible famine settles on the land. In the midst of this crisis, O-lan gives birth to another daughter. She strangles the second girl because there is not enough food to feed the baby and the rest of the family. Wang Lung is forced to take his family to a southern city for the winter. There, O-lan and the children beg while Wang Lung earns money by transporting people in a rented rickshaw. They earn just enough money to eat. Wang Lung begins to despair of ever making enough money to return to his land. He and O-lan briefly consider selling their surviving daughter as a slave. Eventually, a group of poor and desperate people ransacks a rich man's home, and Wang Lung and

O-lan join them. Wang Lung steals a pile of gold coins. With this new wealth, he moves the family back home and purchases a new ox and some seeds. O-lan had stolen some jewels during the looting. Wang Lung allows her to keep two small pearls, but he takes the rest and hurries to buy three hundred acres of Old Master Hwang's land. O-lan gives birth to twins shortly thereafter. The couple realizes that their oldest daughter is severely retarded, but Wang Lung loves the child dearly.

Wang Lung hires laborers to plant and harvest his land. He enjoys several years of profitable harvests and becomes a rich man. When a flood forces him to be idle, he begins to feel restless and bored. He finds fault with O-lan's appearance and cruelly criticizes her for having big feet. He becomes obsessed with Lotus, a beautiful, delicate prostitute with bound feet. Eventually, he purchases Lotus to be his concubine. When O-lan becomes terminally ill, Wang Lung regrets his cruel words and comes to appreciate everything his wife has done for him. Meanwhile, to lessen the demands of his uncle and his uncle's wife, who have moved their family into his house and continued to exploit his wealth, he tricks them into becoming opium addicts. Eventually, Wang Lung rents the Hwangs' house and moves into it with his family, leaving his own house to his uncle's family.

After O-lan's death, Wang Lung's sons begin to rebel against his plans for their life. They do not want to work as farmers and do not have his devotion to the land. Furthermore, his first and second sons often argue over money, and their wives develop an intense animosity toward one another. In his old age, Wang Lung takes a young slave, Pear Blossom, as a concubine. She promises to care for his retarded daughter after his death. In time, Wang Lung is surrounded by grandchildren, but he is also surrounded by petty family disagreements. By the end of the novel, despite Wang's passionate dissent, his sons plan to sell the family land and divide the money among themselves, signaling their final break with the land that made them wealthy.

CHARACTER LIST

Wang Lung The protagonist of *The Good Earth*. He begins life as a poor farmer and marries O-lan, a slave owned by the Hwang family. Wang Lung maintains a fierce attachment to the land. However, he is also extremely ambitious and envies the material success of the wealthy Hwangs. He is increasingly drawn to the Hwangs' decadent lifestyle, and in the end, his piety and love of the land is only partially successful in helping him maintain his good character and moral standing.

O-lan A woman sold to the wealthy Hwang family as a slave when she was ten years old. After she marries Wang Lung, she achieves a respectable position as the mother of three sons. She is a strong, hardworking, resourceful woman and a devoted wife. Still, she is continually marginalized by Wang Lung, and she is eventually replaced in his affections.

Wang Lung's father A traditional and morally severe man.

Wang Lung's uncle A cunning scoundrel and thief. Wang Lung's uncle is the younger brother of Wang Lung's father. Because the uncle is a member of the older generation, Wang Lung must show him respect and give him support in difficult times, despite his despicable nature. The uncle constantly exploits Wang Lung's adherence to traditional Chinese codes of conduct.

The wife of Wang Lung's uncle A village gossip. Like her husband and son, she is lazy and manipulative.

The son of Wang Lung's uncle A wasteful, disrespectful scoundrel, and a sexual predator.

Lotus   A beautiful, delicate prostitute with bound feet. Lotus becomes Wang Lung's concubine. She has a terrible temper.

Wang Lung's first son Extravagant, arrogant, and obsessed with appearances, Wang Lung's first son grows up spoiled and rejects the values that made his father rich.

Wang Lung's second son Crafty, enterprising, and miserly, Wang Lung's second son is more responsible than the first son, but he also rejects his father's traditional values as outmoded.

The wife of Wang Lung's first son The daughter of a local grain merchant, Liu. She grew up in a wealthy family, so she urges her husband to spend money on luxury items; she is spoiled and reckless. Like many women from wealthy families, she has bound feet.

The wife of Wang Lung's second son The daughter of a modest landowning village family. She becomes enemies with the wife of Wang Lung's first son.

Wang Lung's third son The twin of Wang Lung's second daughter. He dreams of glory and becomes a soldier against his father's wishes.

Wang Lung's first daughter Suffers from severe malnutrition as an infant during a famine year. She is retarded and never learns to speak. Wang Lung develops a strong attachment to her and worries about what will become of her after his death.

Wang Lung's second daughter The twin of Wang Lung's third son. After Wang Lung begins to criticize O-lan's appearance cruelly, especially her big feet, O-lan decides to bind the little girl's feet. Wang Lung promises her in marriage to Liu's son.

Cuckoo   A slave who worked in the House of Hwang at the same time as O-lan. Cuckoo was beautiful in her youth, so the Old Master took her as his concubine while O-lan worked as a kitchen slave. Arrogant and bad-tempered, she insulted and berated O-lan constantly.

Ching   Wang Lung's neighbor in the village and, later, Wang Lung's capable, faithful, valued servant.

Pear Blossom A slave purchased by Wang Lung during the famine years, when she was seven years old. She serves as Lotus's personal servant for years.

Liu   A grain merchant in town and a relative of Wang Lung's by marriage.

Old Mistress Hwang The opium-addicted matriarch of the great Hwang family.

Old Master Hwang The patriarch of the great Hwang family when Wang Lung is a poor farmer. He spends money extravagantly and drains his coffers by taking a succession of concubines.

CHARACTER LIST

ANALYSIS OF MAJOR CHARACTERS

WANG LUNG

The protagonist of *The Good Earth,* Wang Lung begins the novel as a poor, simple young farmer forced to marry a slave, and ends it as a wealthy patriarch with enough money and influence to own concubines. Though he gains a fortune, Wang partially loses his connection to the earth, his simple piety, and his ability to participate in the old traditions that have given his life meaning. His success is, therefore, a mixed blessing.

Throughout the novel, Wang's character is essentially defined by two contrasting and even contradictory traits. The first trait is his love of the land, which enables his piety, his good sense, his frugality, his work ethic, and his love of family. The second trait is his desire for wealth and status. Though Wang's love of the land keeps his heart pure for much of the novel, his acquisitiveness and desire for status eventually sullies his character and darkens his actions. Though in the end Wang's moral sense causes him to repent his separation from the land, he never quite loses his tendency to desire wealth and status, and he passes on this tendency to his sons. Consequently, in his old age, he is doomed to watch them repeat the mistakes of the Hwangs and sever their connection from the land that created their fortune.

O-LAN

In many ways the strongest and most memorable character in *The Good Earth,* O-lan exemplifies the situation of women in traditional China and the sacrifices they had to make in order to adhere to cultural notions of feminine respectability. O-lan spends her life working for an endeavor for which she never sees a reward: she gives all her effort and applies all her considerable capability to improving Wang Lung's position, and she receives neither loyalty nor passion from him in return. He is annoyed when she becomes pregnant with her second child, fearing that her condition will keep her from working in the fields, and later he has no qualms about cruelly insulting her unbound feet and taking her treasured pearls to give to his concubine. O-lan spends much of the novel in the position of victim, but she gains a great deal of dignity in the reader's eyes by stolidly and uncomplainingly enduring her husband's behavior. It is O-lan who makes many of the hardest decisions in the novel—smothering her infant daughter to spare food for the family, for instance—and she bears these hard decisions with admirable fortitude.

Because O-lan is so reticent, silence being a quality that is highly valued in wives in Wang Lung's culture, Buck uses means other than speech to indicate the extent of O-lan's inner pain. For instance, on her wedding night, O-lan unconsciously flinches away from Wang Lung, which suggests that she has been abused as a slave in the House of Hwang. O-lan never complains about Wang Lung's cruelty in insulting her feet—but she does immediately begin binding her daughter's feet, warning her daughter not to complain of the pain for fear of angering Wang Lung. We see the extent of O-lan's bravery when she makes no complaint for years and years about the grave illness that swells her belly. O-lan represents the dignity and courage of the marginalized wife.

WANG LUNG'S OLDEST SON

Wang Lung's oldest son is in many ways similar to Wang Lung himself. The primary difference is that Wang Lung was raised in poverty, and his son is raised in luxury. Like Wang Lung, the oldest son is focused and ambitious—but whereas Wang Lung only desires to obtain wealth and respectability, his son desires to become a great scholar and live a life of splendor. Wang Lung and his son both show outward signs of respecting their elders, but while Wang Lung truly believes in the custom of filial piety, his son merely pays it lip service, not truly caring about the needs of the older generation. This difference in their respect for elders is an example of the general difference between Wang Lung and his son: Wang Lung retains his connection to tradition even while craving wealth and advancement, whereas his son has no interest in what he considers quaint and outmoded ethical ideas, and feels free to live only for himself.

THEMES, MOTIFS & SYMBOLS

THEMES

MAN'S RELATIONSHIP TO THE EARTH

The overarching theme of *The Good Earth* is the nourishing power of the land. Throughout the novel, a connection to the land is associated with moral piety, good sense, respect for nature, and a strong work ethic, while alienation from the land is associated with decadence and corruption. Buck's novel situates this universal theme within the context of traditional Chinese culture. Wang Lung, a farmer, has an intimate relationship with the earth because he produces his harvest through his own labor. In contrast, the local Hwang family is estranged from the earth because their wealth and harvests are produced by hired labor. Buck suggests that Wang Lung's reverence for nature is responsible for his inner goodness, as well as for his increasing material success, and that the decadent, wasteful ways of the wealthy are due to their estrangement from the land. Buck also suggests throughout the book that while human success is transitory, the earth endures forever. These ideas about the earth give the novel its title.

WEALTH AS A DESTROYER OF TRADITIONAL VALUES

The basic narrative form of *The Good Earth* has an upward trajectory: as Wang Lung's fortunes rise, he becomes more decadent and more similar to the amoral Hwang family, whose fall parallels his own rise. It is the wealth of the Hwangs that enables them to loosen their ties to the land, hire laborers and spend their own days in idleness and leisure. In this climate, vice takes root and thrives, as the Old Master becomes obsessed with debauchery and the Old Mistress becomes addicted to opium. As Wang Lung becomes wealthier, he too is able to hire laborers, and he becomes obsessed with women such as Lotus. He begins to fund his uncle's opium addiction, and at last he buys the house of the Hwangs and

moves into it. As Wang Lung's children grow older, it becomes clear that being raised in the lap of luxury has severely eroded their own sense of duty to their father, their respect for the land, and the religious observances on which Wang Lung and his father base their lives.

In this way, Wang Lung's life story is a case study of how traditional values erode under the influence of wealth. But Buck does not attribute this erosion solely to the corrupting influence of wealth, or at least not solely to the *individual* experience of wealth. The new ideals of Wang Lung's sons demonstrate the changing nature of Chinese culture. Buck suggests that the modernization of China, itself a function of wealth, creates cultural conflicts.

THE OPPRESSION OF WOMEN IN CHINESE CULTURE
Primarily through the character of O-lan, Buck explores the position of women in traditional Chinese culture, focusing on the hardships and limitations faced by women, from abuse in childhood to servitude in adulthood. Although she was a lifelong feminist, Buck takes a cool, neutral tone toward the oppression of women in China, choosing to focus on individual experience rather than to make large-scale political or social claims. She presents in an unbiased manner the practices of foot-binding, female infanticide, and selling daughters as slaves, constantly drawing attention to the circumstances that would impel a woman to commit such actions without ever endorsing the actions themselves. She also suggests that husbands who take concubines and work their wives like slaves are not necessarily cruel men, but people behaving as their society mandates. Her criticism is directed less toward particular acts committed by individual characters than toward the larger cultural values that produce and allow those acts to occur.

Buck's feminism is implicit in her portrayal of O-lan. Through O-lan, Buck emphasizes the crucial economic contributions women make to their families. She also uses O-lan to suggest that, ironically, the more women are able to help, the less men place sexual and romantic value on them.

THEMES

MOTIFS

> *Motifs are recurring structures, contrasts, and literary devices*
> *that can help to develop and inform the text's major themes.*

BIRTH, DEATH, AND THE CYCLE OF NATURE

Buck draws parallels between the natural cycle of growth, death, and regeneration and the rise and fall of human fortune and human life. When O-lan gives birth to her first two sons, for instance, she immediately returns to tending the fields, which connects the creation of human life to the bounty of the earth. Similarly, the droughts, floods, and famines that ruin the earth's harvest are metaphorically linked to death and downfall.

RELIGION

Wang Lung's religious observance serves as a measuring stick of his mindset. When Wang Lung feels a strong connection to the earth and when his fortunes are good, he is extremely pious and frequently shows signs of faith in the earth god (as when, for instance, he burns incense to celebrate his marriage to O-lan). When his connection to the earth is weak and when his fortunes decline, he often reacts with bitterness toward the gods and does not outwardly worship them (as when he refuses to acknowledge their statues when he moves his family south during the famine). When Wang is in a period of transition, as when his fortunes are changing, he is often anxious about the gods and prays frequently to them to preserve his good luck.

SYMBOLS

> *Symbols are objects, characters, figures, and colors used to*
> *represent abstract ideas or concepts.*

FOOT-BINDING

In traditional Chinese culture, small feet were considered an attractive female trait. The custom of binding young girls' feet to ensure that their feet would remain small was practiced for almost a thousand years, from the tenth century to the Communist takeover of mainland China in 1949. Foot-binding was usually begun when a girl was between the ages of five and seven. Her mother would fold all her toes except her big toe beneath her foot, then tightly wrap a thick bandage at least several feet in length around the foot, so tightly that it actually prevented the bones from growing and eventually caused the foot to fold in half. The ideal product of foot-binding was known as a lotus foot, a foot that, on a grown woman, was not more than three inches long.

Foot-binding was extremely painful, and the pain lasted throughout a woman's life—though the pain lessened as she grew older because her foot was essentially dead. Today, the process would be considered nothing short of torture: apart from the crushing pain of retarded bone growth, the process caused the nails of the four folded toes to grow into the soles of the feet. It also caused an extremely bad odor as various parts of the foot died. Foot-binding made it nearly impossible for a woman to walk for any substantial length, and even a short walk was excruciatingly painful.

Despite the brutality of this practice, it was widespread throughout China, and by 1900 only the poorest and most wretched girls did not have their feet bound. Bound feet were considered so much more attractive than unbound feet that, without bound feet, it was very difficult for a girl to find a husband. Throughout *The Good Earth,* Buck uses foot-binding as a symbol for the moral depravity of wealth, which would subject young girls to torture simply to make them more attractive to men. Attraction to foot-binding also serves as a symbol of Wang Lung's longing for wealth and status. He is initially disappointed to discover that O-lan's feet are not bound, even though her unbound feet enable her to work in the fields with him, which dramatically increases his family's fortune. Nevertheless, though she was an outspoken advocate against the practice, Buck takes a very objective, neutral tone toward foot-binding in *The Good Earth,* drawing attention to the cultural tendencies that might make a woman choose to do such a thing to her daughter. When O-lan binds her own daughter's feet, for instance, she is motivated by Wang Lung's rejection of her, by his criticism of her "large" unbound feet, and by her desire for her daughter to have a happy marriage with a husband who loves her.

THE HOUSE OF HWANG

The House of Hwang is a symbol of wealth, extravagance, decadence, and downfall throughout the novel, a constant reminder of wealth's corrosive effect on morality and long-term success. As the site of the Old Mistress's opium addiction, the Old Master's whoring, and the young lords' abuse of slaves, the house is a palpable sign of disconnection from the land and of narcissistic self-absorption. When Wang Lung buys the House of Hwang after O-lan's death, the transaction is a grim symbol of his own family's fall from grace, represented by his children's decision to sell his land and live in splendor in the Hwangs' house.

O-LAN'S PEARLS

The pearls, which O-lan steals in the revolt in Chapter 14 and which Wang Lung allows O-lan to keep, are an important symbol of the love and respect Wang Lung affords his wife. Though O-lan does not say so, it is clear that she treasures the pearls as proof of her husband's regard for her. When Wang Lung takes the pearls away from her and gives them to the prostitute Lotus, it is as though he is taking away his love and respect. O-lan is inwardly devastated, and the incident symbolizes the extent to which wealth and idleness have corrupted the once admirable Wang Lung.

Summary & Analysis

Chapter 1

Summary

Wang Lung, a poor farmer in rural China, has recently reached the age for marrying. His father wants to find him a suitable wife and approaches the prosperous Hwang family to ask whether they can spare a slave for Wang Lung. Wang Lung's father insists that the woman be unattractive. He worries that a pretty girl would have attracted the young lords of the house and would therefore have lost her virginity. Wang Lung sees the wisdom in this, but he demands that his future wife at least be free of a split upper lip and pockmarks.

On his wedding day, Wang Lung meticulously washes himself. His father complains at the unusual use of so much water. Wang Lung is excited, though, and splurges, paying a man to shave his head and face. He also purchases food for his wedding feast and incense sticks for the gods. Nervousness assails him as he approaches the House of Hwang. The rude, bawdy gate man forces Wang Lung to pay a toll of a precious silver piece before he will allow him inside the gate.

In the House of Hwang, Wang Lung bows before the Old Mistress, who is smoking opium. The Old Mistress calls for Wang Lung's bride, who is named O-lan. O-lan is tall and sturdy, and her face is smooth and brown. Wang Lung is disappointed that her feet are not bound. The Old Mistress states that her family purchased O-lan at the age of ten during a famine year. The Old Mistress believes O-lan is a virgin. Before letting the couple leave, she asks that O-lan bring her first child to see her.

On the walk home, Wang Lung carries O-lan's heavy box and purchases some peaches for her. When they reach the house, he goes to the small temple on his family's fields to burn incense in honor of the earth god and his lady. Wang Lung's father complains about the expenses for the wedding feast, but he is secretly pleased that there will be guests. O-lan prepares the meal, but she refuses to be seen by other men until her marriage is consummated. Her modesty and her good cooking please Wang Lung greatly.

ANALYSIS

The first chapter of *The Good Earth* sets up a contrast between the poor, simple Wang Lung and the wealthy, powerful Hwang family. The decadent, opium-filled Hwang house is also a warning and a foreshadowing of the pitfalls of wealth that will seduce Wang Lung and his offspring. The Hwangs are a family of moral decay and narcissism.

Buck contrasts Wang Lung's knowledge of nature to the Hwang family's disrespect for their land. As a poor farmer, Wang Lung has an intimate relationship with the earth: having no money for workers, he must personally plant and harvest his crops, and as a result, he spends a great deal of time in the fields, alone with nature. His religion is based on worshipping the earth deity, for whom he burns incense before the wedding feast. This offering indicates Wang Lung's recognition that the land is more powerful than he is. Because of this recognition, Wang Lung is frugal, hardworking, and modest. Conversely, because the Hwang family is rich, its members do not personally involve themselves in the labor from which they derive their riches. Instead, they hire laborers and buy slaves to work for them. Hiring others to do their work means they have become estranged from their land. The Hwangs worship wealth and the material goods wealth can buy, rather than recognizing that their wealth is derived from the land and subject to the land's whims. For this reason, they have become careless with their money. They occupy their time with idle pleasures, spending money on expensive items, such as rich foods, opium, drink, and women.

Buck represents traditional Chinese culture, including the inferior position accorded to women, as objectively as possible. Buck, a lifelong feminist, does not overtly criticize the traditional role of Chinese women, but she is frank in her depiction of the difficulties women endured because of that traditional role. Her depiction of O-lan's experiences makes these difficulties clear. Like O-lan, Chinese women had no real rights, no voice in choosing their spouses, and no means of meeting their husbands before the day of their marriage. The early interactions between O-lan and Wang Lung show that some women lived in constant fear. Although Wang Lung treats her kindly, carrying the heavier burdens and buying her fresh spring peaches, O-lan is filled with fear because she does not know what to expect from him next. And, as Buck subtly indicates, O-lan has endured unpleasantness from men. When Wang Lung wakes her to take her to bed on their wedding night, O-lan instinctively defends herself from a blow before realizing that it is her husband waking her. This behavior indicates that O-lan was probably physically abused as a slave, also a common practice in traditional Chinese culture.

CHAPTERS 2–4

SUMMARY: CHAPTER 2

> *There was only this perfect sympathy of movement,*
> *of turning this earth of theirs over and over to the*
> *sun, this earth which formed their home and fed their*
> *bodies and made their gods.*
>
> *(See* QUOTATIONS, *p. 43)*

The morning after his wedding night, Wang Lung suddenly wonders whether his new wife likes him. When she brings him a bowl of tea, a luxury for a poor farmer, he rejoices that she seems to feel kindly toward him. Wang Lung settles into married life with contentment and pleasure. O-lan proves to be resourceful and hardworking. She keeps his small house immaculate and mends all of the family's clothing. She rarely speaks, however, and Wang Lung wonders at the fear and sadness in her eyes. When their home is in order, O-lan begins working in the fields with Wang Lung. Soon after their marriage, O-lan announces that she is pregnant. Though Wang Lung tries to accept the news calmly, he is filled with a deep inner joy.

SUMMARY: CHAPTER 3

O-lan refuses to have anyone attend her during her labor and specifically bans anyone from the House of Hwang. She explains that she does not want to see anyone from the Hwang family until she can introduce her son to the Old Mistress. She plans to dress herself and her baby well for the occasion. She tells her husband exactly what she and the baby will wear to the Hwang house and what they will do there. Wang Lung is amazed that O-lan has already imagined their child so clearly. Wang Lung, his father, and O-lan are delighted when O-lan gives birth and the baby is a boy.

SUMMARY: CHAPTER 4

Wang Lung purchases a pound of red sugar for his wife and new son. In addition, he purchases fifty eggs and dyes them red, a sign for all to see that his new child is a boy. Finally, he buys four sticks of incense to burn in honor of the earth god.

Soon after the child's birth, O-lan returns to working in the fields, stopping when necessary to nurse her child. The harvest is extraordinarily good. Wang Lung has such bounty that he can store some until midwinter, knowing that in the winter, people will pay high prices for grain. On the one-month anniversary of the child's birth, Wang Lung holds a celebration and gives out his red boiled eggs. This celebration is a small extravagance, but Wang Lung and O-lan are generally frugal people. O-lan makes the family's shoes and repairs damaged items instead of purchasing new ones. The couple hides the silver they have begun to accumulate in a hole in the wall.

ANALYSIS: CHAPTERS 2–4

Buck draws parallels between the rise and fall of families and the cycles of the natural world—the harvest's beginning and end is compared to birth and death. She suggests that just as the seasons change, great families come and go, and fortunes rise and fall. Wang Lung's family, which works hard and loves the land, is entering its springtime, while the Hwang family, which is materialistic and extravagant, is entering its autumn, and nothing is unchangeable but the earth itself.

The idea that all human life begins and ends in the unchanging earth is the bedrock of the novel, as well as the source of its title. The novel repeatedly insists that the land deserves respect and that those who do not accord it this respect will eventually fall on hard times.

Buck's portrayal of Chinese culture remains objective and understated in tone throughout these chapters. In traditional Chinese culture, the silence of women was highly valued, and O-lan, a conscientious woman, is almost always silent. But even though we learn almost nothing about O-lan's character from her speech, we learn a great deal about her through her actions. She shows her pleasure with Wang Lung by bringing him hot tea in the morning. She shows her great pride in her home by taking care to make it look the best it can; she cleans and mends household items before joining Wang Lung in the fields. Her actions establish her as extraordinarily capable, hardworking, and resourceful. Buck hints at dark episodes in O-lan's past, as evidenced by O-lan's unexplained refusal to allow anyone from the House of Hwang attend her during her labor.

Buck's characterization of O-lan demonstrates the importance that Chinese culture ascribed to women's labor. O-lan's labor is crucially important to Wang Lung, for with her help, he is able to produce a huge harvest and lay the foundations for future success.

O-lan's skill at laboring makes Wang Lung's initial disappointment by her unbound feet seem foolish, since O-lan would not be able to work in the fields with the tiny, painful feet produced by foot-binding. Wang Lung initially desired a wife with bound feet to prove that he had enough money to support a wife whose feet prevented her from working. Of course, without a wife capable of laboring, he never would have gained the wealth this status symbol was supposed to represent. Buck shows that Wang Lung, despite his love of the land, has a dangerous weakness for the trappings of wealth.

CHAPTERS 5–6

SUMMARY: CHAPTER 5

In observance of the New Year, Wang Lung buys red squares of paper printed with letters symbolizing happiness and wealth, and pastes them all over his home and farm equipment. O-lan prepares moon cakes for the holiday, similar to those eaten in the House of Hwang. O-lan plans to take the best moon cakes and give them to the Old Mistress when she goes to the Hwang house to present her new son.

Dressed in new clothes, Wang Lung and O-lan take their baby son and the cakes to the House of Hwang. The gate man is duly impressed with how O-lan and Wang Lung have fared. O-lan leaves her husband and goes to visit. While Wang Lung waits, the gate man's wife gives him tea. He hardly acknowledges her and does not drink the tea, pretending the leaves are not of the high quality he is used to. When O-lan returns, she tells Wang Lung that their baby is more beautiful and better dressed than any of the Old Master's children. She also reports that the Hwang family has struggled and that for the first time in her memory the slaves and the Old Mistress do not have new coats for the New Year, as she herself does. A cook told O-lan that the family spends money recklessly: the Old Master keeps taking more concubines, and the Old Mistress is addicted to opium.

Hearing about the Hwangs' difficulties and thinking about the rise in his own fortunes fills Wang Lung with joy. He rejoices in his mind about how well he has done and how lucky he is to have such a beautiful son. Realizing that he has been displaying his joy, Wang Lung becomes fearful that evil spirits will steal his fat, attractive son. To protect the child, he laments out loud that it is too bad that their firstborn is a girl with smallpox.

When O-lan mentions that the Old Mistress told her the Hwangs must sell some of their land, Wang Lung resolves to buy it.

SUMMARY: CHAPTER 6

After bribing the Hwangs' agent, Wang Lung purchases the small parcel of land. He is happy to own this new land, but he must now work much harder to tend his fields. When O-lan becomes pregnant, he is irritated rather than glad, since he believes she will be unable to work during the harvest season. However, irritation gives way to happiness when O-lan gives birth to a second son and returns to the fields to work. Wang Lung has another good harvest, and again he has silver to spare.

ANALYSIS: CHAPTERS 5–6

The idle, decadent Hwangs pursue women and drugs, and their fortune slides. In contrast, the hardworking Wang Lung continues to prosper. In Chapter 5, the gatekeeper serves as a gauge for how far Wang Lung has come since marrying O-lan: on Wang Lung's first visit to the Hwangs' house in Chapter 1, the gatekeeper mocks him and demands a bribe before letting him in; now, the gatekeeper is visibly impressed with Wang Lung's new suit and invites him in for a cup of tea. Similarly, Wang Lung was originally overawed by the spectacle of the house; now, however, he does not drink the tea brought to him by the gate man's wife, as if the tea is not good enough for him.

Buck ascribes Wang Lung's success to his continuing devotion to the land, and the Hwangs' decline to their distance from it. When Wang Lung buys a parcel of land from the Hwangs, it both proves that he is growing richer and suggests that he wants to return his wealth to the land. Still, Wang Lung has begun to show subtle signs of change, and as his dream of material success comes true, he begins to lose some of his honest, simple frugality. We see this change in Chapter 5, when he behaves rudely to the gate man's wife; it is perhaps most evident, however, in his gradually changing treatment of O-lan.

Buck presents an evenhanded picture of O-lan's life. O-lan recognizes her good luck in marrying Wang Lung and shows her gratitude by being the perfect wife. She knows that her marriage brought her out of slavery and that Wang Lung is a kindhearted man who treats her well. Because she has become a wife and a mother of sons, her social status has improved, and she can depend on her sons to support her in her old age. Yet even in this fine situation, O-lan is constantly marginalized. Once the novelty of marriage wears off, Wang Lung begins to take O-lan for granted. In Chapter 6, for example, he is annoyed when she becomes pregnant, because it removes her from the fields. O-lan is an ideal wife, seldom complaining and always devoted, but Wang Lung does not appear to notice this.

O-lan does not outwardly complain about her former life as a slave. However, she seems pleased to hear of the Hwangs' troubles, and she delights in presenting her son to the Old Mistress and proving that her social status has improved since she lived as a slave. However, Buck suggests that even in victory, O-lan must succumb to the dictates of a patriarchal world, for had O-lan given birth to a girl, she never could have taken pride in her daughter.

CHAPTERS 7–9

SUMMARY: CHAPTER 7
Wang Lung chastises his uncle's wife for letting her daughter, who is of marriageable age, run free in the streets. The uncle's wife complains that they have no money for a dowry. O-lan gets pregnant again, and when she becomes sick, Wang Lung works the fields alone. One day, his uncle approaches Wang Lung for money. Unable to restrain himself, Wang Lung criticizes the laziness of his uncle and his family. His uncle slaps him for insulting an elder and threatens to tell the whole village. To placate him, Wang Lung loans him the money, ostensibly to pay for a matchmaker for his daughter.

The quarrel with his uncle makes Wang Lung concerned that his run of good luck is over, and when O-lan gives birth to a daughter, Wang Lung worries that this unlucky event—unlucky because the baby is not a son—is another omen of impending unhappiness.

SUMMARY: CHAPTER 8
The rains are late in coming, and the drought destroys most of Wang Lung's crops. The drought drives the House of Hwang further into financial ruin, and Wang Lung is able to purchase a tract of land from the Hwangs that is twice as large as the last one. His own troubles, however, are not over: the harvest is scanty, and O-lan is pregnant for the fourth time. Finally, hunger forces Wang Lung to kill his work ox for food. His uncle complains to the villagers about how little food his nephew gave him, alerting the villagers that Wang Lung has money and food stored away. One day, a group of desperate villagers, convinced that Wang Lung is hiding a fortune, bursts into Wang Lung's home and steals his small store of food. When they try to steal the furniture, O-lan chastises them because they dare to criticize Wang Lung when they themselves have not sold

their own furniture. Ashamed, the thieves slink away from Wang Lung's house carrying with them the little food they could find.

SUMMARY: CHAPTER 9

A famine settles across the land. Wang Lung's neighbor Ching reports that some people are eating human flesh. Ching took part in the attack on Wang Lung's home, and now, feeling guilty, he gives Wang Lung a handful of beans. O-lan gives birth to another daughter. This time, she strangles the baby so that it will not be an impossible burden on the family. Wang Lung goes to bury the tiny corpse, but a ravenous dog lies in wait to eat the body and refuses to leave. So weak from hunger that he is almost unable to support himself, Wang Lung leaves the body to the dog. Wang Lung's uncle comes with men from town to ask Wang Lung to sell some of his land; the uncle thinks that he can force Wang Lung into selling for a low price, even though the uncle himself gave Wang Lung a great deal of advice about the importance of helping one's relatives. Wang Lung refuses, but he does sell them his furniture. In despair over the death of his infant daughter and the disloyal behavior of his uncle, Wang Lung decides that the only way for the family to survive is to move south, away from the famine.

ANALYSIS: CHAPTERS 7–9

As Wang Lung's previously good fortunes take a turn for the worse, Buck underscores the differences between Western and Chinese cultural values, asking her Western readers to understand how moral values and desperate circumstances might drive the novel's characters to act as they do. It might seem strange to Western readers, for instance, that Wang Lung lets his lazy, wasteful uncle exploit him. However, in traditional Chinese culture, respect for the elder generation and filial piety are extremely important values. Wang Lung has been raised with these values, and he recognizes that his society will judge him harshly if he breaks with tradition. He must allow himself to be exploited by his uncle if he wants to maintain his reputation within the community.

It might also seem unthinkable that O-lan could bear to kill her daughter. However, both circumstances and cultural values lessen the horror of her choice. She has two sons and an older baby daughter, and the family is suffering from desperate poverty. The baby will likely die of malnourishment eventually anyway, and to feed it would take food out of the mouths of her husband and children.

Just as the threat of starvation drives Wang Lung's neighbors to raid his home, the same threat drives O-lan to kill her own child. Culturally, too, whereas it was unthinkable to kill a male infant, killing a female one was a common practice. This does not excuse O-lan's deed, but it shows that there was a social precedent for it. Buck was a lifelong critic of the Chinese practice of killing female infants, but she was also aware that poor Chinese families facing starvation do not have the luxury of refusing all but the morally acceptable path.

The famine that reduces Wang Lung to grinding poverty provides a glimpse of the hard life facing poor farmers in old China. The drought is also a reminder that the earth is the only constant force in the world. For all of his hard work, Wang Lung is subject to the whims of nature. The novel's large theme is that the fortunes of humanity are transitory compared to the earth's permanence.

CHAPTERS 10–13

SUMMARY: CHAPTER 10
Carrying his old father on his back, Wang Lung makes his way through the town with his family. As he walks through the town, Wang Lung is bitter at the gods for their failure to help him, and refuses to turn to acknowledge the statues commemorating the gods. He hears of a "firewagon," or train, that can take his family south more quickly than they could walk. Everywhere in town, crowds are assembling to go south in search of food. Outside the crumbling House of Hwang, a tattered group of starving men curses the Hwangs, who drink wine while people are starving. Wang and his family join the throng traveling to the train station, and though Wang Lung distrusts the loud, massive firewagon, he and his family board the train and travel away from the village.

SUMMARY: CHAPTER 11
On the train, Wang Lung tries to learn what life will be like in the south. Some men teach him how to beg, but Wang Lung is distraught at the prospect of begging and hopes that he will be able to find work. When they reach their destination, Wang Lung's family purchases mats to build a hut and goes to the public kitchens to buy cheap rice gruel. They are forbidden to carry any of the food home out of concern that the wealthy are using it to feed their pigs. O-lan and the two boys are forced to earn money by begging. Wang Lung finds a job pulling a rickshaw, and, with effort, he is able to earn enough money to feed his family. Over time, he learns how

to haggle for a good price. At first the family is discouraged. Even though Wang Lung works and the others beg, they can do no more than earn enough money to eat. They feel like foreigners in their own country until they see the Westerners living in the city, who are more foreign than they are.

SUMMARY: CHAPTER 12

Wang Lung hears young men in the streets speaking about the necessity of revolution. The city is filled with signs of wealth, yet there is a despairing multitude of people who live on the border of starvation. O-lan has begun to allow the children to steal, knowing that this may be the only way they can get enough food. One day Wang Lung returns home to find his wife cooking a piece of pork, the first piece of meat they have had since killing their ox. However, when his younger son brags that he stole the meat, O-lan is upset. He allows his family to eat the pork, but will not eat it himself. After dinner, he beats his son for stealing. Wang begins to long for a return to his home and the land.

SUMMARY: CHAPTER 13

The older poor people in the city accept their lot without complaining, but the young men are growing restless. They increasingly speak of revolt. O-lan is again pregnant. When planting time approaches, the family does not have the money to go home or buy seed. Wang Lung is desperate to leave the city and return home, and he tells himself that he will be able to do so eventually. O-lan remarks that they have nothing to sell but their daughter. She says she would be willing to sell their daughter into slavery for Wang Lung's sake, since he wants to return home so much. Wang Lung recoils at the thought because he is fond of his daughter. Still, he is tempted by the idea. He moans aloud, torn between his love for his daughter and his love for the land. A man in a nearby hut hears his cry, and they begin talking. The man comments that there are always ways to level the discrepancy between rich and poor. Revolution seems to be in the air.

ANALYSIS: CHAPTERS 10–13

The difficult months in the city strengthen Wang Lung's love of the land and of hard work. Wang Lung has been raised to believe that diligence and frugal living pay off in the end. He is not attracted to the idea of begging; he prefers the backbreaking labor of pulling a

rickshaw around the city. When his sons begin to steal, he is more determined than ever to return to his land and earn an honest living.

As she has done throughout the novel, O-lan once again proves
invaluable in dealing with misfortune. She does not waste time complaining, as Wang Lung does, but quickly educates her children in
the art of begging, even beating the children when they do not beg
effectively. She realizes that if they are to eat and survive, they must
learn to entice pedestrians to part with a few coins.

In these chapters Buck begins to explore the cultural variety of
late-nineteenth- and early-twentieth-century China. Although Wang
Lung and his family travel only a hundred miles from their home, it
is as if they have entered another world. The language is different,
the markets are stuffed with food, political rhetoric abounds, and
the occasional Westerner roams the streets. Turn-of-the-century
China did not have a centralized government, so culture, language,
and economy all differed greatly over short distances. Buck emphasizes this fact by drawing attention to Wang Lung's ignorance of
trains in Chapter 10. Wang Lung's life is so centered on his farm
and village that even the nearby train station seems supernatural
to him. Though he lives in a fairly modern world, Wang Lung and
poor farmers like him have almost no knowledge of social change
or technological innovations.

Although Wang Lung initially knows little of the outside world,
the outside world begins to impose itself on his mind in these chapters, as the seeds of social unrest and violent revolution begin to
sprout all around him. The gap between the rich and the poor in the
city is astonishing. The anger and resentment of the poor is primed
to explode, and the signs are evident long before the explosion finally happens in Chapter 14. The rich try to hold off rebellion by
providing cheap rice gruel for the poor in public kitchens, but this
tactic is effective for only so long. The city is full of young men
longing for revolution: "The scattered anger of their youth became
settled into a fierce despair and into a revolt too deep for mere words
because all their lives they labored more severely than beasts, and
for nothing except a handful of refuse to fill their bellies." This poverty and anger foreshadows the revolutionary explosion that eventually occurs, as well as the intense social upheaval that takes place
in China during later decades.

CHAPTERS 14–16

SUMMARY: CHAPTER 14

> *But Wang Lung thought of his land and pondered this*
> *way and that, with the sickened heart of deferred hope,*
> *how he could get back to it.*
>
> *(See* QUOTATIONS, *p. 43)*

One day, a Western missionary gives Wang Lung a paper. Wang Lung is illiterate and cannot read the words printed on it. His father looks at the paper, which is printed with a picture of a man nailed to a crosspiece, and states that the man must have been evil to have met such a fate. O-lan uses the paper to line her family's ragged shoes. Another man hands Wang Lung a paper depicting a fat man stabbing a thin man dressed in rags. A man giving a speech states that the fat man represents the rich and the capitalists, and the thin man represents the poor. Wang Lung snorts at the man's speech since he views land, rather than money or food, as the only lasting thing. He saves the paper for repairing shoes.

Soldiers begin forcibly conscripting poor men into the army. Wang Lung does not know what the fighting is about or who the combatants are. The rich begin transporting their goods out of the city. The markets empty out and the public kitchens close. Wang Lung again considers selling his daughter. Worried for his daughter's safety, he asks O-lan if she was beaten in the House of Hwang. She replies, in a passionless monotone, that she was beaten every day with a leather thong. When he asks her if pretty girls were beaten, she replies in a long speech that not only were they beaten, but from the time they were children, they were raped by the lords of the house, sometimes by different lords in one night.

As Wang Lung wonders what to do with his daughter, the enemy invades the city, and the impoverished multitude ransacks the houses of the rich. Wang Lung participates in the looting and comes away with a stash of gold coins. He is thrilled, because the gold will provide him with the means to return home.

SUMMARY: CHAPTER 15

Hunger makes thief of any man.
(See QUOTATIONS, *p. 44)*

Wang Lung purchases some seed and an ox and returns home. There, he discovers that his house has been ransacked. Ching informs Wang Lung that some bandits, rumored to be affiliated with Wang Lung's uncle, lived in Wang Lung's house during the winter. Ching's wife has died, and he gave his daughter to a soldier rather than see her starve. Wang Lung gives Ching some seed to plant his land and offers to plow it for him. He wants to repay Ching for the handful of beans Ching gave him months before. Wang Lung learns that his uncle sold all of his daughters.

Wang Lung is not disheartened about the dilapidated state of his house; it will be easily mended, and his land is still the same. Excited about their renewed prosperity, but worried about bad luck, Wang Lung and O-lan buy incense sticks to burn for the gods.

SUMMARY: CHAPTER 16

Wang Lung discovers that O-lan stole some jewels during the looting in the south. Because she had lived in a wealthy house, she knew where the rich hid their treasures. Wang Lung declares that they should buy more land with the jewels. O-lan asks to keep only two small pearls, and Wang Lung agrees. When he goes to the House of Hwang to inquire about buying more land, Wang Lung is amazed to find that only the Old Master and a slave, Cuckoo, still live there. Over the course of his discussion with the slave, who is running the place, he learns that bandits raided the house, taking the slaves and the goods, and that the Old Mistress died from shock during the furor of the attack. Wang Lung uses the jewels to purchase three hundred acres of the Old Master's land.

ANALYSIS: CHAPTERS 14–16

In Chapter 14, Buck lampoons the absurdity of the Christian missionary project. In general, the Western missionaries are unaware of the bleak reality facing the impoverished masses. They have no idea of the prices of things or the appropriate amount of money to give to beggars. They are far too wealthy and too remote to appreciate the anguish and suffering felt by the poor. They are also profoundly ignorant about Chinese culture; their missionary project is merely a form of cultural imperialism. The paper depicting the crucifixion symbolizes this almost complete lack of actual communication between the two cultures. Wang Lung cannot read it, but he does realize the value of paper for mending shoes. Here, Buck strongly implies that missionaries would better spend their energies by attending to the economic needs of the Chinese poor rather than to any perceived spiritual needs.

Although Buck was a fierce opponent of the practice of selling female children as slaves, she is also realistic about the social conditions facing poor Chinese families. Though O-lan is fully aware of the abuse her daughter will potentially face as a slave, she must consider the option of selling her. If the daughter were to remain with the family, all of them might starve. If she is sold to a wealthy family, she will be provided with food and shelter, and her sale will give the family money to survive. Also, O-lan considers selling her daughter because she sees how desperately her husband wants to return to the land. This willingness to please him demonstrates her steadfast adherence to the customs that mandate loyalty from wives. Buck does not criticize O-lan for considering selling her daughter into slavery, just as Buck did not criticize O-lan for smothering her younger daughter during the famine. Instead, Buck criticizes a society that creates the desperation that requires such behavior.

Wang Lung is forced to compromise his own values during the raid on the rich man's house; he becomes a thief, even though in the previous chapter, he beat his son for stealing. Just as O-lan's desperation partly explains her willingness to sell her daughter, Wang Lung's extremely dire situation may excuse his momentary hypocrisy: his family is facing starvation. The futility of living many long months in poverty have made Wang Lung more realistic about what he needs to do to provide for his family. He has begun to do what it takes to survive, with less regard for the traditional values to which he felt connected when he worked the land. Ironically, his urban-minded, anti-traditional theft allows him to return to the honest rural life he reveres.

Because Wang Lung has raided another man's house, he now understands why Ching stole from him with the rest of the villagers. Thus, he forgives Ching, gives him seed, and offers to plow his land. Buck asks the reader to learn, as Wang Lung does, that desperation can force even the most moral people to compromise their values.

CHAPTERS 17–19

SUMMARY: CHAPTER 17

Wang Lung buys more livestock and builds new rooms for his house. He purchases Ching's land and invites him to live with the family and work for them. The land is so extensive that Wang Lung must hire more laborers, and he puts the trustworthy Ching in charge of them. O-lan gives birth to twins, a boy and a girl. Because he has enough money to care for more children, Wang Lung is delighted at the birth of the twins. Wang Lung's first daughter does not talk or do those things normal for a child her age, and Wang Lung realizes she is retarded. He is relieved that he never sold her, because she would have been killed once her owners learned of her disability. He becomes more attached to the little girl because of his guilt over almost selling her, and he takes her to the fields with him.

Wang Lung enjoys a number of good harvests and stores enough food and money to tide the family over in bad years. He lives a life of success. He builds a new house. Ashamed of his own illiteracy, Wang decides to send his oldest son to school. The second son, who is always quick to complain, whines that he wants to go to school too, and Wang Lung agrees. At school, the boys are called Nung En and Nung Wen. *Nung* means "one whose wealth is from the earth."

SUMMARY: CHAPTER 18

When a flood prevents Wang Lung from planting his fields, he finds himself idle and restless. His laborers take care of everything that needs to be done. One day, he looks at O-lan as if for the first time and finds her a "dull and common" creature, not fit to be the wife of a wealthy landowner. Although he knows he is hurting her and wants to stop, he cruelly criticizes her appearance, especially her large, unbound feet. O-lan does not get angry, but looks scared and hides her feet. Wang Lung's guilt about what he has done makes him angrier, especially when he recalls that he would have none of his new wealth if O-lan had not stolen the jewels and given them to him when asked.

He goes to the old tea shop, which used to impress him. Now, however, it looks cheap in his newly wealthy eyes and makes him impatient. A little nervously, he goes to the extravagant new tea shop. The opulent surroundings astonish him, especially the pictures of beautiful women on the walls, which he assumes are "women in dreams." After spending day after day there, he discovers that Cuckoo, the beautiful woman who worked as a slave in the Hwang house with O-lan, works there. A masterful businesswoman, she teases him for only drinking tea in the teahouse instead of enjoying wine or women. Cuckoo tells him that the pictures on the wall are of real women, and that he can have any woman he chooses. Wang decides he prefers a beautiful young girl painted holding a lotus flower, but he leaves the tea shop without telling Cuckoo of his decision.

SUMMARY: CHAPTER 19

> *O-lan returned to the beating of his clothes and when*
> *tears dropped slowly and heavily from her eyes she did*
> *not put up her hand to wipe them away.*
>
> *(See* QUOTATIONS, *p. 44)*

Wang returns to the tea house unsure of what he will do. When Cuckoo sees him approaching, however, she says scornfully, "Ah, it is only the farmer!" Stung, Wang Lung angrily shows her a handful of silver. She quickly takes him upstairs to Lotus. When he sees the beautiful young girl, with her tiny hands and "apricot eyes," he becomes mesmerized by her. He admits to her that he is a sexual novice, and she must teach him everything. After their first encounter, he returns to her every day, never able to satiate his thirst for her. His interest in Lotus changes Wang Lung completely. Lotus thinks Wang Lung's ponytail is old-fashioned, so he cuts it off, much to O-lan's dismay. He loses interest in farming. He buys new clothing, takes a special interest in his appearance, and spends money extravagantly. Eventually, although what he is doing makes him sick, he demands O-lan's two pearls, planning to give them to Lotus.

ANALYSIS: CHAPTERS 17–19

Buck had a severely retarded daughter, so her portrait of Wang Lung's affection for his retarded child was likely influenced by her own feelings for her daughter. We do not learn the exact reason for Wang Lung's daughter's retardation, though Wang Lung wonders if the severe malnutrition she suffered as a baby caused it. Wang Lung's fierce attachment to his daughter is unusual: a retarded daughter is a lifelong burden because she will not marry and cannot contribute economically to her own family.

Throughout this section, the increasingly wealthy, increasingly decadent Wang Lung begins to resemble the Hwangs as they were at the zenith of their wealth. This transformation has been foreshadowed by Wang's obvious desire for material success and by his admiration of the trappings of wealth, such as women with bound feet. At last he achieves his goal of accumulating a great fortune: his wealth equals what the Hwangs' once was. But in becoming wealthy, he begins to fall prey to the same decadent practices that eventually destroyed the Hwangs. His wealth creates as many problems as it solves, but Buck does not seem to imply that wealth alone causes these problems. Rather, it is the idleness and moral decay that often comes with wealth that is at the root of Wang Lung's difficulties.

As long as Wang Lung maintained an intimate relationship with the land, he continued to live his life according to sound moral principles. However, when made idle by the flood, he starts to contemplate his image and his social status. He looks at O-lan as a possession and finds her unworthy of a rich man. He realizes he is rich in the first place only because of the help that O-lan has given him, both with her jewels and with her constant work and support. Even this realization, however, does not stop him from becoming enamored with possessions and another woman.

Lotus symbolizes Wang Lung's shift from revering principles like hard work and frugality to revering sensual pleasures. Lotus is described entirely in terms of physical objects: her nails are the "color of lotus buds," her laughter is like a "silver bell," and her hand is "like a fragile dry leaf." For Wang Lung, she is not a true person but "the painted picture of a woman." Lotus's sensual, one-dimensional existence contrasts with O-lan, who is depicted as fully human. Buck writes not of O-lan's likeness to physical objects but of her inner qualities: kindness, selflessness, loyalty, and determination. The women's feet provide a miniature summation of their differences. Lotus's bound feet, like Lotus herself, serve a purely decorative function, whereas O-lan's unbound feet allow her to work for her family.

Buck emphasizes the healing power of the earth in Wang Lung's life by connecting his downfall to a time when he is kept from working the land. She hints that Wang will be able to restore his good sense by giving himself back to the earth. The fact that the first word of his sons' names at school means "one whose wealth comes from the land" suggests that Wang Lung should recall that he owes his good fortune to the land.

SUMMARY & ANALYSIS

CHAPTERS 20–22

SUMMARY: CHAPTER 20

Wang Lung's uncle returns, once more banking on his ability to exploit Wang Lung's filial piety. Wang Lung's uncle and the uncle's wife and son move into Wang Lung's house. His uncle's wife, seeing Wang Lung's new attention to his appearance, declares that Wang Lung hungers for another woman. She tells O-lan to accept that all men with the necessary wealth buy additional wives. Upon hearing this, Wang Lung is emboldened and asks his uncle's wife to act as his agent and help him purchase Lotus. He tells his uncle's wife that he will do anything to have Lotus for his own, including sell his land. Waiting to hear whether Lotus will come, Wang Lung is in agony. He lashes out at O-lan for not brushing her hair. She bursts into tears "as he had never seen her weep before, even when they starved, or at any other time." She tells him that she has borne him sons. Wang Lung is suddenly ashamed, because he knows he has no real grounds for complaint against O-lan.

He builds a separate court and fishpond, and installs Lotus there with Cuckoo as her servant. Lotus is carried to the house on a chair; because of her bound feet, she is unable to walk long distances. Wang Lung is satisfied once she is there and has sex with her every night.

SUMMARY: CHAPTER 21

Although O-lan ignores Lotus, she vents her unhappiness by speaking out against Cuckoo. She states that Cuckoo was cruel to her when they were both slaves in the House of Hwang, and Cuckoo was a higher-ranking slave than she. O-lan refuses to do anything for Cuckoo now since O-lan is the first wife in this household. She will not let Cuckoo work in the kitchen. When Wang Lung tries to force O-lan to be civil to Cuckoo, O-lan brings up the pearls that Wang Lung took from her to give to Lotus. Silenced, Wang Lung decides to build another kitchen for Lotus and Cuckoo to alleviate the hostility. Cuckoo spends extravagantly on delicate, expensive foods for her mistress. To Wang Lung's dismay, his uncle's wife befriends Cuckoo and Lotus. Wang Lung's passion for Lotus begins to wane.

Wang Lung's father, who is getting senile, sees Lotus one day and cries out that there is a "harlot" in the house. He does not accept any explanation for her presence and begins to annoy Lotus as a child would, spitting on her floor and throwing stones in her fishpond. One day, the twins take their retarded sister into Lotus's court. Upon seeing Lotus's brightly colored clothing and jewelry, the girl tries to touch them. Lotus screams, bringing Wang Lung hurrying to her side. She rails against the "idiot" and insults his children. Angered by her words, Wang Lung does not visit Lotus for two days. When he goes to her again, she tries especially hard to please him. He forgives her, but he "never [loves her] again so wholly as he had loved her."

One day, Wang Lung goes outside and sees that the fields are ready for plowing. He casts off his elegant clothes and cries out for his hoe and plow. Buck writes, "A voice cried out in him, a voice deeper than love cried out in him for his land."

SUMMARY: CHAPTER 22

Wang Lung throws himself into work. He loses his unhealthy obsession with Lotus, so she ceases to have the power to manipulate him easily. Wang Lung's eldest son reads and writes well, and Wang Lung is very proud of him. Eventually, however, the eldest son becomes moody and irritable. When the son begins skipping school, Wang Lung beats him. Later, O-lan informs Wang Lung that she saw a similar moodiness in the young lords in the House of Hwang. Usually, the matter was solved by giving them a female slave. Wang Lung is surprised, but O-lan tells him that their son is not like them—since he is never forced to work, he has time to feel sorry for himself. Wang Lung is secretly pleased at the idea that his son is as spoiled as a lord and decides that it is time to find a wife for him.

ANALYSIS : CHAPTERS 20–22

Wang Lung's sudden disregard for O-lan's valuable contributions to his wealth can be understood to some extent in relation to patriarchal Chinese society. As a woman, O-lan is not considered an equal partner in their marriage but a valuable piece of property whose worth is measured by Wang Lung's satisfaction with her. Probably because she too considers it a natural state of affairs for Wang Lung to desire a second woman, O-lan, despite her obvious pain at being supplanted by Lotus, continues to behave as the model Chinese wife.

However, O-lan begins to stand up for herself more and more. She points out that she has given her husband three healthy sons. Her implication, which he understands, is that she has been a model wife, that she has done the most important thing a wife can do in giving him sons, and that he has no legal complaint against her. When angered, O-lan reminds Wang Lung of his cruelty in taking her pearls from her.

But until the floods subside, Wang Lung shows little regard for O-lan's, or anyone else's, opinion. Throughout the previous chapters, Wang Lung demonstrated an intense sensitivity to the opinions of others, but now that he is idle and wealthy, his focus turns inward. He is no longer happy with the mere ownership of money; now he wishes to behave and look like a rich man. O-lan compares him to the dissolute and extravagant Old Master Hwang. She means it as an insult, but Wang Lung takes it as a compliment. He is also pleased when O-lan tells him that their son is just like a spoiled young lord.

Even at his worst, however, Wang Lung does not stray entirely from the moral values that defined his upbringing. As the reigning male in his household and a rich man, he is within his rights to take a concubine. Indeed, some or most people would consider taking a concubine the natural and proper course for a man in his position. However, Wang Lung, who grew up distrusting the values of the wealthy, is uneasy with his actions. For this reason, he is embarrassed when his father finds out about Lotus. Moreover, when his son reaches sexual maturity and begins to struggle with sexual longing, Wang Lung cannot bring himself to buy a female slave for him, a common and accepted practice for rich families. Instead, he resolves to find a wife for his son.

Wang Lung's return to working the land after the floods subside brings about his moral and emotional renewal, as he begins to lose interest in Lotus and return to the simpler ethic of hard work that Buck connects to happiness and success throughout the book.

CHAPTERS 23–25

SUMMARY: CHAPTER 23

Wang Lung does not want to marry his son to a village woman. However, he is not friendly with the rich men in town, so he cannot approach them. Lotus tells him about Liu, a grain merchant who visited her in the tea house and who has a daughter nearly of marriageable age. Soon after, Wang Lung learns that his uncle's son took Wang Lung's son to an old prostitute in town. Wang Lung is angry and goes to the prostitute to offer her twice her usual fee if she turns his son away instead of sleeping with him. He tells Cuckoo to begin marriage negotiations with Liu right away. Meanwhile, he furiously demands that his uncle and his uncle's family leave. His uncle opens his coat and shows him a false red beard and a piece of red material, the symbols of a notorious band of robbers who rape women and burn men alive. His uncle dares Wang Lung to expel him.

Wang Lung realizes why only his home has been spared in the frequent raids over the years. If he evicts his uncle now, his house will be plundered. If he goes to the courts to report his uncle, he reasons, it is more likely that he will be beaten for disloyalty than that his uncle will be prosecuted. He allows his uncle to stay and gives silver to his uncle's wife and son.

Cuckoo succeeds in arranging the betrothal. However, Liu's daughter is only fourteen, and Liu wants to wait three years before the wedding. In the midst of these troubles, a plague of locusts descends, and Wang Lung must battle to save his crops.

SUMMARY: CHAPTER 24

Wang Lung refuses his oldest son's request to go to a university in the south. For three years, O-lan's belly has been swollen as if she is pregnant, although she is not. When asked how she is, she tells of pain in her stomach. However, she still works, because Wang Lung has never offered to buy her a servant. One day, O-lan goes to her husband's room and tells him that their eldest son often visits Lotus alone. He does not believe her, and she advises him to come home unannounced one day, and see. Wang Lung discovers his son alone with Lotus one day. He beats both of them and immediately sends his son to the university in the south.

SUMMARY: CHAPTER 25

Wang Lung's second son is a crafty, intelligent boy, so Wang Lung approaches Liu to ask if he will accept the boy as his apprentice. Liu gladly agrees, and they tentatively discuss the possibility of a marriage between Liu's son and Wang Lung's second daughter. When Wang Lung returns home, he is pleased to see that his daughter's foot-binding is working. However, there are tears on her cheeks. She explains that the binding hurts and that she has not mentioned it because O-lan cautioned her not to weep aloud or Wang Lung might end the foot binding. She tells her father that O-lan said that if her feet are not bound, her husband will not love her, just as Wang Lung does not love O-lan. Wang Lung is stung with guilt at these words. He tells Cuckoo to finalize the betrothal of his second daughter, and he decides to train his third son as a farmer, but as he makes these decisions he is thinking about his wife.

Wang Lung is filled with remorse for his lack of concern for O-lan. He notices that her movements are painful and slow. He orders her to bed and hires a doctor. Under Chinese law, a doctor cannot promise to heal a patient if he cannot be sure of his success. Hence, the doctor names an exorbitant fee for healing O-lan as a means of gently telling Wang Lung that his wife cannot be saved. When Wang Lung goes to the kitchen "where O-lan had lived her life for the most part," he cries.

Analysis: Chapters 23–25

Wang Lung's misunderstanding of his eldest son is partly due to their vastly different upbringings. They are alike in some respects, especially in their ambition. However, having grown up with money, Wang Lung's oldest son desires social prestige more than simple wealth. Whereas Wang Lung wanted his sons educated so that they would not be scorned by grain merchants, his son wants to go to a great university in the south so that he can see other places and learn from true scholars. Wang Lung and his son are both sensitive to the opinions of others; they are both obsessed with appearances. The son's luxurious upbringing merely amplifies the traits that he shares with his father.

Because of his difficulties with his oldest son, Wang Lung resolves to try different approaches with his younger sons. He takes his second son out of school and makes him an apprentice to Liu. Wang Lung hopes that exposure to a practical trade will prevent the restlessness and desire for social prestige that plague his older son. Moreover, he wants his third son to be a farmer like himself, because his third son respects the earth's healing power. He wants the entire family to stay close to the earth because he thinks that estrangement from the earth caused the Hwang family's decline.

The words of Wang Lung's daughter awaken Wang Lung to the guilt he bears for causing O-lan to suffer. He is also made uncomfortably (and perhaps somewhat unrealistically) aware of the suffering of women in his culture. Wang Lung realizes that bound feet cause pain. He also realizes that O-lan has been such a boon to him precisely because she did not have bound feet.

When Wang Lung discovers that his wife is dying, he is heartsick. Buck describes the kitchen as the place where O-lan spent her life to

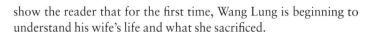

show the reader that for the first time, Wang Lung is beginning to understand his wife's life and what she sacrificed.

CHAPTERS 26–27

SUMMARY: CHAPTER 26

O-lan lies sick for months. Only now that she is bedridden does the family realize how important she was to the household. Wang Lung stays at her bedside during her long illness and is kind to her. Sometimes, in her fever, O-Lan speaks as if she is a terrified slave at the Hwangs, or calls out for her parents. O-lan asks that her son's betrothed come and tend her. She does, and O-lan and Wang Lung are pleased with the girl's good behavior. O-lan makes a final request: she wants to see her son married before dying. Liu agrees, although this will mean his daughter will marry a year earlier than planned. When his son returns from the south, Wang Lung is pleased to see that he has grown into a man. During the elaborate wedding ceremony, the young man appears happy with his father's choice of a bride. O-lan is too weak to attend the ceremony, but she lies in bed listening. Soon after the wedding, O-lan dies. Her last words are a fevered insistence that "beauty will not bear a man sons," and that even if she is ugly, she has borne sons for her husband.

Soon after her death, Wang Lung's father passes away. O-lan and Wang Lung's father are buried during one funeral ceremony. As Wang Lung walks away after the ceremony, he has one thought: that he cannot bear to see Lotus wear the two pearls he took from O-lan.

SUMMARY: CHAPTER 27

After a flood brings a terrible famine, Wang Lung carefully monitors household expenses. Although he treats his uncle's family like honored guests, they complain about his miserly ways. Wang Lung's oldest son becomes angry, seeing the way his uncle's family takes advantage of his father. He also feels he must guard his wife from his cousin's roving eye. Wang Lung explains that he cannot refuse his uncle's demands because his uncle is a member of a notorious band of robbers. His son suggests that they drown the entire family. When Wang Lung refuses, his son suggests that he buy opium for them; opium is very expensive, but if the uncle and cousin become addicted to it, keeping them supplied with opium will be less costly than paying for their current expenses. Wang Lung is reluctant to try this plan until his uncle's son tries to molest his younger daughter.

He sends the girl to live with her future husband's family because he fears he cannot protect her virginity. Afterward, he purchases six ounces of opium for his uncle's family in an effort to make them addicted.

ANALYSIS: CHAPTERS 26–27

With the knowledge that O-lan's death is imminent, Wang Lung must again confront his cruel treatment of her. He gives her comfort by letting her know that she will be respectably buried and mourned. O-lan has always taken pride in knowing that she rose from her position as a lowly, ugly kitchen slave to become the mother of a rich man's three sons. On her deathbed, she relishes pointing out this rise to Cuckoo. Her dying insistence that her great achievement in life is being the mother of sons demonstrates that O-lan continues to be the ideal wife and mother.

Although Wang Lung has treated his wife without the great respect she deserves, he is kind to her as she is dying. He still does not feel he loves her, however, even though he wants to and feels guilty that he does not. He sits by her bedside, and "[w]hen he took this stiff dying hand he did not love it, and even his pity was spoiled with repulsion towards it." Buck portrays his lack of love for her not as a moral failure, but as something he cannot help. Because Wang Lung is saddened and ashamed of his own failure to love his wife, he does not seem cruel.

Although Wang Lung has good reason to try to subdue his evil uncle, his decision to trick his uncle and his uncle's wife into becoming opium addicts is another sign of the Wangs' increasing similarity to the Hwang family. Wang Lung originally was horrified to find that the Old Mistress was an addict, because he considered opium addiction an expensive, wasteful, and decadent habit. For all his reverence of family, however, Wang Lung is willing to turn his relatives into opium addicts.

Wang Lung's oldest son's willingness to drown his uncle's family reveals that he lacks the familial reverence that is so important to Wang Lung. His suggestion that his father kill a relative of an older generation is a serious breach of society's moral dictates. Again, Buck implies that wealth and idleness lead to moral corruption and to a change in the cultural pattern of respect for elders.

CHAPTERS 28–34

SUMMARY: CHAPTER 28

Wang Lung's uncle and his uncle's wife eagerly accept the opium Wang Lung buys for them. They quickly become addicted and no longer trouble Wang Lung. Refugees return from the south and borrow money at high interest from Wang Lung to buy seed. Many are forced to sell some of their land to Wang Lung in order to do so, while others sell their daughters. They prefer selling their daughters to Wang Lung than to any other landowner, for they know Wang Lung is kind. When a man brings Pear Blossom, his small seven-year-old girl, Wang Lung buys her as a servant for Lotus. His uncle's son does not become an opium addict and continues to idle around the house, eyeing whatever women pass by, including the wife of Wang Lung's oldest son. Wang Lung's oldest son comes up with the suggestion that Wang Lung rent the old great house of the Hwang family and allow the family of Wang Lung's uncle to stay in the present house. Wang Lung's second son supports the idea, and Wang Lung rents the house. Although he did not even know he wanted it, Wang Lung is deeply satisfied to live in the house that for him always epitomized wealth and success.

SUMMARY: CHAPTER 29

Wang Lung's second son, who has never struck his father as interested in marriage, astonishes Wang Lung by expressing a well-considered desire to marry a hardworking, frugal village woman from a landed family. Wang Lung readily agrees, and his second son is betrothed to a woman recommended by Ching. Soon after, and to everyone's delight except his mother's, the uncle's son decides to go join a war in the north. Wang Lung continues to adjust to the lifestyle of the rich: he purchases new clothing for his family and slaves, he sleeps late, and he takes a liking to expensive foods. Wang Lung's daughter-in-law, the wife of his oldest son, gives birth to a healthy son. Wang Lung's son hires a wet nurse for the child because he doesn't want to see his wife's breasts ruined and her energy drained.

Soon after the baby is born, the eldest son suggests that they set up tablets of their ancestors to worship during feast days, as other great families do. In the midst of all this happiness, Ching dies suddenly in the fields. Wang Lung prepares an elaborate funeral and insists that his family wear clothing of mourning. He wants to bury Ching near his father and O-lan, but he cedes to his son's requests not to bury a servant with the family. Wang Lung walks in the fields less frequently, because his fields remind him of his faithful servant.

SUMMARY: CHAPTER 30

At his eldest son's urging, Wang Lung allows the purchase of expensive furniture and decorations. He gets so careless about the cost of these purchases that he refuses to finance them only when his responsible second son complains of the excessive expense. Wang Lung learns that his third son does not want to be a farmer; reluctantly, Wang Lung hires a tutor for him. Wang Lung entrusts the family finances to the second son. In time, Wang Lung's uncle dies and is buried in the family plot.

SUMMARY: CHAPTER 31

The battlefront of the war moves closer, and the son of Wang Lung's uncle, now a soldier, exploits Wang Lung's hospitality to house himself and some of his comrades. Meanwhile, Cuckoo suggests they allow Wang Lung's cousin to pick a slave for himself. He asks for Pear Blossom, but Pear Blossom begs to be spared. Another slave offers to take her place, and the arrangement is sealed. When Wang Lung's cousin departs, the slave is pregnant.

SUMMARY: CHAPTER 32

The slave gives birth to a girl, and Wang Lung marries the slave to one of his laborers. Meanwhile, his uncle's wife dies and is buried in the family plot. Tension between the two older brothers increases. They argue over money, and their wives become enemies. Wang Lung's third son announces that he would like to be a soldier, and Wang Lung offers him anything he desires if he will change his mind. However, when the son asks for Pear Blossom, Wang Lung is overcome with jealousy. He says that his son may not have children by the slaves, as it is immoral.

SUMMARY: CHAPTER 33

One night, Pear Blossom confesses to Wang Lung that she does not like young men because they are too "fierce," whereas old men are kind. Wang Lung takes her for his concubine. Furious at this, the third son leaves his father's house to go fight in the war.

Summary: Chapter 34

> *Now, evil, idle sons — sell the land! ... If you sell the*
> *land, it is the end.*
>
> *(See* QUOTATIONS, *p. 45)*

As Wang Lung nears the end of his life, he gives Pear Blossom some poison and asks that she feed it to his retarded daughter when he dies. He fears that no one will care for his daughter in his absence and thinks it would be kinder to kill her than to let her suffer. Pear Blossom says she cannot kill her and promises to take care of his daughter after he dies. As Wang Lung ages, he becomes more and more senile. His children and grandchildren find his beliefs and attitudes about life humorously old-fashioned. He takes pleasure in his food and drink and in Pear Blossom. He feels he is dying, and asks his sons to buy a coffin. They do, and the coffin comforts Wang Lung. He moves to the earthen house with the coffin, saying he would like to spend his dying days there. One day he overhears his two elder sons discussing the sale of some of the land. He cries out, "If you sell the land, it is the end," and although the sons assure him over and over that they will not sell the land, they smile at each other over Wang Lung's head.

Analysis: Chapters 28–34

Though Wang has found moral redemption in working on his land, his family has its own momentum and comes to resemble the Hwang family. Even Wang Lung exploits the desperation of the returning refugees, purchasing their land at low prices and extracting high interest rates on their loans. This creates further hardship and forces many families to sell their daughters as slaves for extra money. With his newfound wealth, Wang Lung betrays the morals he had upheld during his impoverished youth. None of his three sons respects the land as the source of wealth and happiness. Each becomes attracted to various vanities: prestige, money, and military glory.

Wang Lung's move into the Hwang family's old home symbolizes his family's complete usurpation of the Hwang family's place in the world. Living in the Hwang house gives Wang Lung "satisfaction he had longed for all his days without knowing it." His oldest son wants to increase their status as a great family still further by turning to ancestor worship. With this change, Wang Lung's family ceases to venerate the land; they now venerate only themselves. Their estrangement from the land is not just physical, but spiritual as well.

Buck implies that larger social developments are eroding traditional Chinese values. As the revolt in the city in Chapter 14 indicated, social unrest has been increasing over the years, and signs of modernization have begun to appear in Chinese society. Wang Lung's third son becomes an officer in the revolutionary army. This is probably a reference to the emerging Communist movement in early twentieth-century China, a serious challenge to the traditional structure of Chinese society. When the son of Wang Lung's uncle returns to exploit Wang Lung yet again, the son does not even bother to make a show of appealing to traditional filial piety. He relies on the brute force of his soldiers and gets exactly what he wants. Buck may be implying that force is taking the place of traditional values.

In taking Pear Blossom as his concubine, Wang Lung once again repeats the behavior of Old Master Hwang, who spent his last years with young concubines. However, in this and in his other actions, Wang Lung's transformation is not complete. He is not exactly like the Old Master. For example, Wang Lung is somewhat ashamed of taking a mistress who is so young, and asks Pear Blossom again and again if he is not too old for her. He is a kind and gentle master to his servants, and men come to him when they must sell their daughters. His judgment is respected, and people ask him for advice. Wang Lung, although he has repeated some of the mistakes of the Hwangs, is a good and honest man.

Buck paints the fortunes of Wang Lung's family as no different from the fortunes of any other family. Families, like the seasons, follow a cycle, and Buck suggests that Wang Lung's sons will likely ruin themselves by abandoning the land. The novel ends bleakly, as Wang Lung, the wisest and best man in his family, is condescended to by his wealthy, foolish sons.

IMPORTANT QUOTATIONS EXPLAINED

1. There was only this perfect sympathy of movement, of turning this earth of theirs over and over to the sun, this earth which formed their home and fed their bodies and made their gods . . . Some time, in some age, bodies of men and women had been buried there, houses had stood there, had fallen, and gone back into the earth. So would also their house, some time, return into the earth, their bodies also. Each had his turn at this earth. They worked on, moving together—together—producing the fruit of this earth.

This quotation from Chapter 2 describes Wang Lung's and O-lan's connection to the land. Buck emphasizes the cyclical nature of the earth. The repeated motions of "turning this earth of theirs over and over" parallels the image of people, homes, and fortunes rising up and falling back into the earth over and over again. This quotation is important as an early explanation of Wang Lung's ethical and spiritual connection to the land, and also as an emphasis on the recurring motif of the earth's permanence compared to the fleeting lives and fortunes of human beings.

2. But Wang Lung thought of his land and pondered this way and that, with the sickened heart of deferred hope, how he could get back to it. He belonged, not to this scum which clung to the walls of a rich man's house; nor did he belong to the rich man's house. He belonged to the land and he could not live with any fullness until he felt the land under his feet and followed a plow in the springtime and bore a scythe in his hand at harvest.

This quotation from Chapter 14 depicts when Wang Lung, now in the city, looks back on his land with longing. His connection to the simple life of the earth has been affirmed by his time in the poverty-stricken urban chaos of the city. This quotation is important because it shows Wang Lung thinking in terms of economic comparisons. He has always had a tendency to think of money, but this tendency has been strengthened by his experience of acute poverty in the city. His longing for the tangible connection to his land provided by the plow and scythe—the symbols of planting and harvest, and of effort and reward—also indicates the acute loneliness he feels.

3.   Hunger makes thief of any man.

This quotation from Chapter 15 is spoken by one of the villagers who knows of the looting of Wang Lung's house. It comes as Wang Lung is fresh from his participation in the looting of the rich man's house in Chapter 14. Eventually, he forgives Ching for his part in looting Wang Lung's house during the famine. Wang Lung has learned from his own experience that the desperate conditions of poverty and starvation can force even the most upright individual to compromise his moral belief in the interest of sheer survival, and as a result he no longer holds a grudge against Ching. Instead, he chooses to remember Ching's kindness to Wang Lung's family. It is here that the enduring friendship between Wang and Ching begins.

The forgiving sentiment of the quotation, which shows a willingness to think of morality in relative terms, characterizes Buck's attitude toward her characters throughout the book. When Wang understands the conditions that led to Ching's behavior, he is able to understand and empathize with Ching. This attempt to understand is the same attitude Buck takes toward such practices as slavery, infanticide, and foot-binding, and it is the approach that *The Good Earth* asks its readers to take as well.

4.   Then slowly she thrust her wet wrinkled hand into her
      bosom and she drew forth the small package and she gave
      it to him and watched him as he unwrapped it; and the
      pearls lay in his hand and they caught softly and fully the
      light of the sun, and he laughed. But O-lan returned to
      the beating of his clothes and when tears dropped slowly
      and heavily from her eyes she did not put up her hand to
      wipe them away; only she beat the more steadily with her
      wooden stick upon the clothes spread over the stone.

This heartrending passage from Chapter 19 comes as Wang Lung demands that O-lan give him the pearls that she had stolen from the rich man's house, which he allowed her to save. The pearls were an important symbol of Wang Lung's respect and consideration for his wife; now, however, he is in love with the young prostitute Lotus, and he wants to give the pearls to her as a gift. Completely disregarding O-lan's feelings, Wang is oblivious to the agony he causes her with this demand. Wang laughs at the beauty of the pearls while the reticent O-lan, too conscientious to complain about this bad treatment, weeps softly to herself. That O-lan continues to do her domestic chores as she weeps emphasizes the unending work she does without complaint, only to be repaid with Wang Lung's indifference and condescension.

5. Now, evil, idle sons—sell the land! . . . It is the end of a
   family—when they begin to sell the land . . . Out of the
   land we came and into it we must go—and if you will hold
   your land you can live—no one can rob you of land. . . . If
   you sell the land, it is the end.

Wang Lung makes this speech in Chapter 34, at the end of the novel. He pleads with his sons not to sell his land, and although they assure him they will not, they smile over his head, silently amused at their own deception. Wang Lung's speech is a final plea to honor man's relationship with the land. He attempts with one last speech to make up for the damage his wealth and decadence have done to his sons' perception of the earth's importance. Wang emphasizes again the earth's permanence and its place of central importance in human affairs, but by this point the reader knows his sons will never listen, so that Wang's final words, "If you sell the land, it is the end," grimly and clearly predict the impending downfall of the family Wang's hard work and piety has made rich.

QUOTATIONS

KEY FACTS

FULL TITLE
The Good Earth

AUTHOR
Pearl S. Buck

TYPE OF WORK
Novel

GENRE
Parable, American literature about China

LANGUAGE
English

TIME AND PLACE WRITTEN
1930–1931

DATE OF FIRST PUBLICATION
1931

PUBLISHER
The John Day Company

NARRATOR
The story is narrated in a coolly detached third-person voice that often describes Wang Lung's thoughts and feelings and generally describes only the actions, and not the thoughts, of the other characters.

POINT OF VIEW
The novel is written almost exclusively from Wang Lung's point of view.

TONE
The narrator's tone is solemn and detached. The story is told with a great deal of gravity, but the language is kept very simple and remains placid even when describing events of great trauma and upheaval. The story's tone has reminded some readers of the Bible; it is based in part on the tone of much of the Chinese literature Buck knew well.

TENSE
> Past

SETTINGS (TIME)
> Roughly 1890s–1930s

SETTINGS (PLACE)
> Anhwei, China; Wang Lung's nearby farm; the far-off southern city of Nanking

PROTAGONIST
> Wang Lung

MAJOR CONFLICT
> Wang Lung's desire for wealth and status clashes with his simple respect for the earth and his adherence to old Chinese traditions of religious and filial piety. Later, Wang comes into conflict with his uncle's family and with his children, as they exploit his wealth and disregard his wishes.

RISING ACTION
> The various natural disasters of the book—famine, drought, and flood; Wang Lung's marriage to O-lan and the birth of his children; his struggle through poverty in Kiangsu

CLIMAX
> The financial success of Wang Lung

FALLING ACTION
> Wang Lung's increasing interest in women and sensual pleasures; his old age; the children's decision to sell his land

THEMES
> Man's relationship to the earth; wealth as a destroyer of traditional values; the place of women in Chinese culture

MOTIFS
> The cycle of nature; religion

SYMBOLS
> Foot-binding; the House of Hwang; O-lan's pearls

FORESHADOWING
> The downfall of the Hwangs foreshadows the downfall of Wang Lung's family; the raid on Wang Lung's house and the discovery that his sons have been stealing foreshadow Wang

KEY FACTS

Lung's own theft of the gold from the rich man's house; Wang Lung's disappointment in seeing O-lan's unbound feet foreshadows his affair with Lotus, whose feet are bound.

STUDY QUESTIONS

1. *Why is it ironic that Wang Lung is disappointed that O-lan's feet are not bound?*

Buck's characterization of O-lan demonstrates how important women's labor can be to the financial success of her family. O-lan performs valuable domestic labor, and she increases Wang Lung's wealth by helping him work in the field. For this reason, it is ironic that Wang Lung is disappointed in O-lan's unbound feet. Women with bound feet have difficulty standing and walking and could never perform work such as O-lan's. Wang Lung desires a woman with bound feet as a status symbol, but only through having a wife who could work is Wang Lung able to attain the riches a woman with bound feet was supposed to represent.

2. *Why does O-lan smother the second infant daughter born to her and Wang Lung? To what extent does O-lan's cultural and economic context lessen what might otherwise appear to be a horrible and unforgivable crime?*

It might be tempting to condemn O-lan for smothering her infant, but it is necessary to consider her circumstances. She is already the mother of two sons and a daughter, and the family is living under the burden of a terrible famine; they are in danger of starving to death, and the newborn baby is likely to die a much more painful death by starvation, should she live. O-lan cannot count on having enough nourishment to nurse this baby; should she try to nurse the infant, she might die. Her three young children still depend heavily on her, and it is unlikely that they would survive if she died. Just as the threat of starvation drives Wang Lung's neighbors to raid his home, the same threat drives O-lan to kill her own child.

3.   *Why does Wang Lung endure his uncle's demands?*

It might seem strange to Western readers that Wang Lung would endure his lazy, wasteful uncle's exploitation. However, in traditional Chinese culture, respect for the elder generation is extremely important. Not only was Wang Lung raised with these values, but he recognizes that his society would look down on him were he to break with tradition. He must allow himself to be exploited by his uncle if he wants to maintain his reputation within his community.

How to Write Literary Analysis

The Literary Essay: A Step-by-Step Guide

When you read for pleasure, your only goal is enjoyment. You might find yourself reading to get caught up in an exciting story, to learn about an interesting time or place, or just to pass time. Maybe you're looking for inspiration, guidance, or a reflection of your own life. There are as many different, valid ways of reading a book as there are books in the world.

When you read a work of literature in an English class, however, you're being asked to read in a special way: you're being asked to perform *literary analysis*. To analyze something means to break it down into smaller parts and then examine how those parts work, both individually and together. Literary analysis involves examining all the parts of a novel, play, short story, or poem—elements such as character, setting, tone, and imagery—and thinking about how the author uses those elements to create certain effects.

A literary essay isn't a book review: you're not being asked whether or not you liked a book or whether you'd recommend it to another reader. A literary essay also isn't like the kind of book report you wrote when you were younger, where your teacher wanted you to summarize the book's action. A high school- or college-level literary essay asks, "How does this piece of literature actually work?" "How does it do what it does?" and, "Why might the author have made the choices he or she did?"

The Seven Steps

No one is born knowing how to analyze literature; it's a skill you learn and a process you can master. As you gain more practice with this kind of thinking and writing, you'll be able to craft a method that works best for you. But until then, here are seven basic steps to writing a well-constructed literary essay:

1. *Ask questions*
2. *Collect evidence*
3. *Construct a thesis*

4. Develop and organize arguments
5. Write the introduction
6. Write the body paragraphs
7. Write the conclusion

---

1. ASK QUESTIONS

When you're assigned a literary essay in class, your teacher will often provide you with a list of writing prompts. Lucky you! Now all you have to do is choose one. Do yourself a favor and pick a topic that interests you. You'll have a much better (not to mention easier) time if you start off with something you enjoy thinking about. If you are asked to come up with a topic by yourself, though, you might start to feel a little panicked. Maybe you have too many ideas—or none at all. Don't worry. Take a deep breath and start by asking yourself these questions:

- **What struck you?** Did a particular image, line, or scene linger in your mind for a long time? If it fascinated you, chances are you can draw on it to write a fascinating essay.

- **What confused you?** Maybe you were surprised to see a character act in a certain way, or maybe you didn't understand why the book ended the way it did. Confusing moments in a work of literature are like a loose thread in a sweater: if you pull on it, you can unravel the entire thing. Ask yourself why the author chose to write about that character or scene the way he or she did and you might tap into some important insights about the work as a whole.

- **Did you notice any patterns?** Is there a phrase that the main character uses constantly or an image that repeats throughout the book? If you can figure out how that pattern weaves through the work and what the significance of that pattern is, you've almost got your entire essay mapped out.

- **Did you notice any contradictions or ironies?** Great works of literature are complex; great literary essays recognize and explain those complexities. Maybe the title (*Happy Days*) totally disagrees with the book's subject matter (hungry orphans dying in the woods). Maybe the main character acts one way around his family and a completely different way around his friends and associates. If you can find a way to explain a work's contradictory elements, you've got the seeds of a great essay.

At this point, you don't need to know exactly what you're going to say about your topic; you just need a place to begin your exploration. You can help direct your reading and brainstorming by formulating your topic as a *question,* which you'll then try to answer in your essay. The best questions invite critical debates and discussions, not just a rehashing of the summary. Remember, you're looking for something you can *prove or argue* based on evidence you find in the text. Finally, remember to keep the scope of your question in mind: is this a topic you can adequately address within the word or page limit you've been given? Conversely, is this a topic big enough to fill the required length?

GOOD QUESTIONS

"Are Romeo and Juliet's parents responsible for the deaths of their children?"

"Why do pigs keep showing up in LORD OF THE FLIES*?"*

"Are Dr. Frankenstein and his monster alike? How?"

BAD QUESTIONS

"What happens to Scout in TO KILL A MOCKINGBIRD*?"*

"What do the other characters in JULIUS CAESAR *think about Caesar?"*

"How does Hester Prynne in THE SCARLET LETTER *remind me of my sister?"*

---

2. COLLECT EVIDENCE

Once you know what question you want to answer, it's time to scour the book for things that will help you answer the question. Don't worry if you don't know what you want to say yet—right now you're just collecting ideas and material and letting it all percolate. Keep track of passages, symbols, images, or scenes that deal with your topic. Eventually, you'll start making connections between these examples and your thesis will emerge.

Here's a brief summary of the various parts that compose each and every work of literature. These are the elements that you will analyze in your essay, and which you will offer as evidence to support your arguments. For more on the parts of literary works, see the Glossary of Literary Terms at the end of this section.

LITERARY ANALYSIS

ELEMENTS OF STORY   These are the *what*s of the work—what happens, where it happens, and to whom it happens.

- **Plot:** All of the events and actions of the work.

- **Character:** The people who act and are acted upon in a literary work. The main character of a work is known as the *protagonist.*

- **Conflict:** The central tension in the work. In most cases, the protagonist wants something, while opposing forces (antagonists) hinder the protagonist's progress.

- **Setting:** When and where the work takes place. Elements of setting include location, time period, time of day, weather, social atmosphere, and economic conditions.

- **Narrator:** The person telling the story. The narrator may straightforwardly report what happens, convey the subjective opinions and perceptions of one or more characters, or provide commentary and opinion in his or her own voice.

- **Themes:** The main idea or message of the work—usually an abstract idea about people, society, or life in general. A work may have many themes, which may be in tension with one another.

ELEMENTS OF STYLE   These are the *how*s—how the characters speak, how the story is constructed, and how language is used throughout the work.

- **Structure and organization:** How the parts of the work are assembled. Some novels are narrated in a linear, chronological fashion, while others skip around in time. Some plays follow a traditional three- or five-act structure, while others are a series of loosely connected scenes. Some authors deliberately leave gaps in their works, leaving readers to puzzle out the missing information. A work's structure and organization can tell you a lot about the kind of message it wants to convey.

- **Point of view:** The perspective from which a story is told. In *first-person point of view,* the narrator involves him or herself in the story. ("I went to the store"; "We watched in horror as the bird slammed into the window.") A first-person narrator is usually the protagonist of the work, but not always. In *third-person point of view,* the narrator does not participate in the story. A third-person narrator may closely follow a specific character, recounting that individual character's thoughts or experiences, or it may be what we call an *omniscient* narrator. Omniscient narrators see and know all: they can witness any event in any time or place and are privy to the inner thoughts and feelings of all characters. Remember that the narrator and the author are not the same thing!

- **Diction:** Word choice. Whether a character uses dry, clinical language or flowery prose with lots of exclamation points can tell you a lot about his or her attitude and personality.

- **Syntax:** Word order and sentence construction. Syntax is a crucial part of establishing an author's narrative voice. Ernest Hemingway, for example, is known for writing in very short, straightforward sentences, while James Joyce characteristically wrote in long, incredibly complicated lines.

- **Tone:** The mood or feeling of the text. Diction and syntax often contribute to the tone of a work. A novel written in short, clipped sentences that use small, simple words might feel brusque, cold, or matter-of-fact.

- **Imagery:** Language that appeals to the senses, representing things that can be seen, smelled, heard, tasted, or touched.

- **Figurative language:** Language that is not meant to be interpreted literally. The most common types of figurative language are *metaphors* and *similes,* which compare two unlike things in order to suggest a similarity between them— for example, "All the world's a stage," or "The moon is like a ball of green cheese." (Metaphors say one thing *is* another thing; similes claim that one thing is *like* another thing.)

---

3. CONSTRUCT A THESIS

When you've examined all the evidence you've collected and know how you want to answer the question, it's time to write your thesis statement. A *thesis* is a claim about a work of literature that needs to be supported by evidence and arguments. The thesis statement is the heart of the literary essay, and the bulk of your paper will be spent trying to prove this claim. A good thesis will be:

- **Arguable.** "*The Great Gatsby* describes New York society in the 1920s" isn't a thesis—it's a fact.

- **Provable through textual evidence.** "*Hamlet* is a confusing but ultimately very well-written play" is a weak thesis because it offers the writer's personal opinion about the book. Yes, it's arguable, but it's not a claim that can be proved or supported with examples taken from the play itself.

- **Surprising.** "Both George and Lenny change a great deal in *Of Mice and Men*" is a weak thesis because it's obvious. A really strong thesis will argue for a reading of the text that is not immediately apparent.

- **Specific.** "Dr. Frankenstein's monster tells us a lot about the human condition" is *almost* a really great thesis statement, but it's still too vague. What does the writer mean by "a lot"? *How* does the monster tell us so much about the human condition?

GOOD THESIS STATEMENTS

Question: In *Romeo and Juliet*, which is more powerful in shaping the lovers' story: fate or foolishness?

Thesis: "Though Shakespeare defines Romeo and Juliet as 'star-crossed lovers' and images of stars and planets appear throughout the play, a closer examination of that celestial imagery reveals that the stars are merely witnesses to the characters' foolish activities and not the causes themselves."

Question: How does the bell jar function as a symbol in Sylvia Plath's *The Bell Jar*?

Thesis: "A bell jar is a bell-shaped glass that has three basic uses: to hold a specimen for observation, to contain gases, and to maintain a vacuum. The bell jar appears in each of these capacities in *The Bell Jar,* Plath's semi-autobiographical novel, and each appearance marks a different stage in Esther's mental breakdown."

Question: Would Piggy in *The Lord of the Flies* make a good island leader if he were given the chance?

Thesis: "Though the intelligent, rational, and innovative Piggy has the mental characteristics of a good leader, he ultimately lacks the social skills necessary to be an effective one. Golding emphasizes this point by giving Piggy a foil in the charismatic Jack, whose magnetic personality allows him to capture and wield power effectively, if not always wisely."

4. DEVELOP AND ORGANIZE ARGUMENTS

The reasons and examples that support your thesis will form the middle paragraphs of your essay. Since you can't really write your thesis statement until you know how you'll structure your argument, you'll probably end up working on steps 3 and 4 at the same time.

There's no single method of argumentation that will work in every context. One essay prompt might ask you to compare and contrast two characters, while another asks you to trace an image through a given work of literature. These questions require different kinds of answers and therefore different kinds of arguments. Below, we'll discuss three common kinds of essay prompts and some strategies for constructing a solid, well-argued case.

TYPES OF LITERARY ESSAYS

- **Compare and contrast**

  Compare and contrast the characters of Huck and Jim in THE ADVENTURES OF HUCKLEBERRY FINN.

  Chances are you've written this kind of essay before. In an academic literary context, you'll organize your arguments the same way you would in any other class. You can either go *subject by subject* or *point by point*. In the former, you'll discuss one character first and then the second. In the latter, you'll choose several traits (attitude toward life, social status, images and metaphors associated with the character) and devote a paragraph to each. You may want to use a mix of these two approaches—for example, you may want to spend a paragraph a piece broadly sketching Huck's and Jim's personalities before transitioning into a paragraph or two that describes a few key points of comparison. This can be a highly effective strategy if you want to make a counterintuitive argument—that, despite seeming to be totally different, the two objects being compared are actually similar in a very important way (or vice versa). Remember that your essay should reveal something fresh or unexpected about the text, so think beyond the obvious parallels and differences.

- **Trace**

  Choose an image—for example, birds, knives, or eyes—and trace that image throughout MACBETH.

  Sounds pretty easy, right? All you need to do is read the play, underline every appearance of a knife in *Macbeth*, and then list them in your essay in the order they appear, right? Well, not exactly. Your teacher doesn't want a simple catalog of examples. He or she wants to see you make *connections* between those examples—that's the difference between summarizing and analyzing. In the *Macbeth* example above, think about the different contexts in which knives appear in the play and to what effect. In *Macbeth,* there are real knives and imagined knives; knives that kill and knives that simply threaten. Categorize and classify your examples to give them some order. Finally, always keep the overall effect in mind. After you choose and analyze your examples, you should come to some greater understanding about the work, as well as your chosen image, symbol, or phrase's role in developing the major themes and stylistic strategies of that work.

- **Debate**

  Is the society depicted in 1984 *good for its citizens?*

In this kind of essay, you're being asked to debate a moral, ethical, or aesthetic issue regarding the work. You might be asked to judge a character or group of characters (*Is Caesar responsible for his own demise?*) or the work itself (*Is* JANE EYRE *a feminist novel?*). For this kind of essay, there are two important points to keep in mind. First, don't simply base your arguments on your personal feelings and reactions. Every literary essay expects you to read and analyze the work, so search for evidence in the text. What do characters in *1984* have to say about the government of Oceania? What images does Orwell use that might give you a hint about his attitude toward the government? As in any debate, you also need to make sure that you define all the necessary terms before you begin to argue your case. What does it mean to be a "good" society? What makes a novel "feminist"? You should define your terms right up front, in the first paragraph after your introduction.

Second, remember that strong literary essays make contrary and surprising arguments. Try to think outside the box. In the *1984* example above, it seems like the obvious answer would be no, the totalitarian society depicted in Orwell's novel is *not* good for its citizens. But can you think of any arguments for the opposite side? Even if your final assertion is that the novel depicts a cruel, repressive, and therefore harmful society, acknowledging and responding to the counterargument will strengthen your overall case.

5. WRITE THE INTRODUCTION

Your introduction sets up the entire essay. It's where you present your topic and articulate the particular issues and questions you'll be addressing. It's also where you, as the writer, introduce yourself to your readers. A persuasive literary essay immediately establishes its writer as a knowledgeable, authoritative figure.

An introduction can vary in length depending on the overall length of the essay, but in a traditional five-paragraph essay it should be no longer than one paragraph. However long it is, your introduction needs to:

- **Provide any necessary context.** Your introduction should situate the reader and let him or her know what to expect. What book are you discussing? Which characters? What topic will you be addressing?

- **Answer the "So what?" question.** Why is this topic important, and why is your particular position on the topic noteworthy? Ideally, your introduction should pique the reader's interest by suggesting how your argument is surprising or otherwise counterintuitive. Literary essays make unexpected connections and reveal less-than-obvious truths.

- **Present your thesis.** This usually happens at or very near the end of your introduction.

- **Indicate the shape of the essay to come.** Your reader should finish reading your introduction with a good sense of the scope of your essay as well as the path you'll take toward proving your thesis. You don't need to spell out every step, but you do need to suggest the organizational pattern you'll be using.

Your introduction should not:

- **Be vague.** Beware of the two killer words in literary analysis: *interesting* and *important*. Of course the work, question, or example is interesting and important—that's why you're writing about it!

- **Open with any grandiose assertions.** Many student readers think that beginning their essays with a flamboyant statement such as, "Since the dawn of time, writers have been fascinated with the topic of free will," makes them sound important and commanding. You know what? It actually sounds pretty amateurish.

- **Wildly praise the work.** Another typical mistake student writers make is extolling the work or author. Your teacher doesn't need to be told that "Shakespeare is perhaps the greatest writer in the English language." You can mention a work's reputation in passing—by referring to *The Adventures of Huckleberry Finn* as "Mark Twain's enduring classic," for example—but don't make a point of bringing it up unless that reputation is key to your argument.

- **Go off-topic.** Keep your introduction streamlined and to the point. Don't feel the need to throw in all kinds of bells and whistles in order to impress your reader—just get to the point as quickly as you can, without skimping on any of the required steps.

---

6. WRITE THE BODY PARAGRAPHS

Once you've written your introduction, you'll take the arguments you developed in step 4 and turn them into your body paragraphs. The organization of this middle section of your essay will largely be determined by the argumentative strategy you use, but no matter how you arrange your thoughts, your body paragraphs need to do the following:

- **Begin with a strong topic sentence.** Topic sentences are like signs on a highway: they tell the reader where they are and where they're going. A good topic sentence not only alerts readers to what issue will be discussed in the following paragraph but also gives them a sense of what argument will be made *about* that issue. "Rumor and gossip play an important role in *The Crucible*" isn't a strong topic sentence because it doesn't tell us very much. "The community's constant gossiping creates an environment that allows false accusations to flourish" is a much stronger topic sentence— it not only tells us *what* the paragraph will discuss (gossip) but *how* the paragraph will discuss the topic (by showing how gossip creates a set of conditions that leads to the play's climactic action).

- **Fully and completely develop a single thought.** Don't skip around in your paragraph or try to stuff in too much material. Body paragraphs are like bricks: each individual

one needs to be strong and sturdy or the entire structure
will collapse. Make sure you have really proven your point
before moving on to the next one.

- **Use transitions effectively.** Good literary essay writers know
  that each paragraph must be clearly and strongly linked to
  the material around it. Think of each paragraph as a response
  to the one that precedes it. Use transition words and phrases
  such as *however, similarly, on the contrary, therefore,* and
  furthermore to indicate what kind of response you're making.

---

7. WRITE THE CONCLUSION
Just as you used the introduction to ground your readers in the topic
before providing your thesis, you'll use the conclusion to quickly
summarize the specifics learned thus far and then hint at the broader
implications of your topic. A good conclusion will:

- **Do more than simply restate the thesis.** If your thesis argued
  that *The Catcher in the Rye* can be read as a Christian
  allegory, don't simply end your essay by saying, "And that
  is why *The Catcher in the Rye* can be read as a Christian
  allegory." If you've constructed your arguments well, this
  kind of statement will just be redundant.

- **Synthesize the arguments, not summarize them.** Similarly,
  don't repeat the details of your body paragraphs in your
  conclusion. The reader has already read your essay, and
  chances are it's not so long that they've forgotten all your
  points by now.

- **Revisit the "So what?" question.** In your introduction,
  you made a case for why your topic and position are
  important. You should close your essay with the same sort
  of gesture. What do your readers know now that they didn't
  know before? How will that knowledge help them better
  appreciate or understand the work overall?

- **Move from the specific to the general.** Your essay has most
  likely treated a very specific element of the work—a single
  character, a small set of images, or a particular passage. In
  your conclusion, try to show how this narrow discussion has
  wider implications for the work overall. If your essay on *To
  Kill a Mockingbird* focused on the character of Boo Radley,
  for example, you might want to include a bit in your

conclusion about how he fits into the novel's larger message about childhood, innocence, or family life.

- **Stay relevant.** Your conclusion should suggest new directions of thought, but it shouldn't be treated as an opportunity to pad your essay with all the extra, interesting ideas you came up with during your brainstorming sessions but couldn't fit into the essay proper. Don't attempt to stuff in unrelated queries or too many abstract thoughts.

- **Avoid making overblown closing statements.** A conclusion should open up your highly specific, focused discussion, but it should do so without drawing a sweeping lesson about life or human nature. Making such observations may be part of the point of reading, but it's almost always a mistake in essays, where these observations tend to sound overly dramatic or simply silly.

A+ ESSAY CHECKLIST

Congratulations! If you've followed all the steps we've outlined above, you should have a solid literary essay to show for all your efforts. What if you've got your sights set on an A+? To write the kind of superlative essay that will be rewarded with a perfect grade, keep the following rubric in mind. These are the qualities that teachers expect to see in a truly A+ essay. How does yours stack up?

- ✓ Demonstrates a thorough understanding of the book
- ✓ Presents an original, compelling argument
- ✓ Thoughtfully analyzes the text's formal elements
- ✓ Uses appropriate and insightful examples
- ✓ Structures ideas in a logical and progressive order
- ✓ Demonstrates a mastery of sentence construction, transitions, grammar, spelling, and word choice

Suggested Essay Topics

1. *How does Buck satirize Western Christian missionaries in the novel?*

2. *What does Wang Lung's family's gradual disconnection from the land say about their moral position and their hopes for future success? Explain what you think happens to Wang Lung's family after the close of the novel.*

3. *How are Wang Lung and his oldest son alike? Given the similarities in their characters, why do they come into conflict?*

4. *Why does Wang Lung decide to move into the Hwang family's house in town? What does such a move signify for him?*

A+ Student Essay

> In the first part of the novel, Wang Lung pays two
> separate visits to the House of Hwang. How are these
> visits different? How do they illuminate the novel's major
> themes?

In *The Good Earth,* Wang Lung's two early visits to the House of Hwang demonstrate Buck's interest in the social implications of material wealth. When poor, Wang Lung is abused by the Hwangs, but when rich, he is honored and admired. Similarly, throughout the novel, money confers a host of social benefits on Buck's characters: the right to extra attention from salespeople, the right to pretentious titles and honorifics, and the right to treat others as if they are not fully human. By contrast, poor people throughout *The Good Earth* must suffer not only the burdens of frugality but also a sense of diminished status in the eyes of their neighbors. The differences between Wang Lung's trips to the House of Hwang thus introduce Buck's idea that money is not merely a means of acquiring objects: It is a ticket to power and deferential treatment routinely denied to the poor.

By emphasizing the contrast between Wang Lung's two interactions with Hwang's staff, Buck shows that wealth brings the intangible benefits of widespread fear and respect. When Wang Lung is poor, he has no authority over Hwang's gateman, who sneers at his provisions, mocks his marital aspirations, and robs him of a silver coin. He makes no offer to seat and entertain Wang Lung while he awaits Hwang and his family. On the other hand, during Wang Lung's second visit, Wang Lung's obvious wealth and opulent clothes earn him a great deal of deference from the same gateman. The gateman does not demand a silver coin from Wang Lung (who could now easily afford the toll), and he makes the startling offer to serve Wang Lung in his own chambers. Because Wang Lung is rich, he commits the bold act of refusing the gateman's tea, a gesture he would never have considered while poor. Wang Lung's money therefore represents something more than financial clout—it is an excuse to be rude to others and an invitation for awe and kindness from people who would not give a second thought to the poor.

Likewise, many of Buck's wealthy characters emphasize the notion that money has a social dimension, a way of guaranteeing politeness and superior service in a wide range of settings. Shopping for his newborn son, Wang Lung watches as the salesman's eyes drift toward a customer who is better-dressed, and Buck implies that the new customer will receive more attention simply because he is richer. The Old Mistress enjoys more than a sense of greater prosperity in Wang Lung's presence, for her prosperity allows her to criticize Wang Lung's choice of wife, ignore Wang Lung, and ramble tediously about her own future without fear of repercussions. Dressed well, Wang Lung is mistaken for a teacher instead of a lowly farmer and is therefore greeted with respect by an almsman on the street. Again and again, Buck shows that money means more than buying power.

By contrast, Buck's impoverished characters demonstrate that a lack of money is also a lack of status. Though attractive and talented in the kitchen, O-lan is called an ugly woman and a poor cook, because she does not have the money that would guarantee her a basic amount of respect. During the widespread drought, the peasants cannot ask one another, "How are you doing?" but only "How am I doing?" for there seems to be no reason to show kindness to a person when he is not wealthy and well established. The friends of Wang Lung's uncle, who try to buy Wang Lung's land, feel free to mock and swindle their interlocutor because he is poor and therefore powerless. Repeatedly, Buck shows that poverty infects her characters' souls, for it is both a loss of material comfort and a loss of the self-worth and social status that make life bearable.

The two different visits to the Hwang household thus alert us to Buck's interest in the intangible benefits of wealth. Throughout the novel, she will revisit her idea that class difference is more than a matter of economics. The prosperous Wang Lung who takes a courtesan toward the end of his life is infinitely more comfortable and arrogant than the timid, starving Wang Lung who eats dirt during the draught. In Buck's eyes, wealth enacts a transformation that goes far beyond an increase in material possessions, reshaping the very personalities of its owners.

LITERARY ANALYSIS

GLOSSARY OF LITERARY TERMS

ANTAGONIST

> The entity that acts to frustrate the goals of the *protagonist*. The antagonist is usually another *character* but may also be a non-human force.

ANTIHERO / ANTIHEROINE

> A *protagonist* who is not admirable or who challenges notions of what should be considered admirable.

CHARACTER

> A person, animal, or any other thing with a personality that appears in a *narrative*.

CLIMAX

> The moment of greatest intensity in a text or the major turning point in the *plot*.

CONFLICT

> The central struggle that moves the *plot* forward. The conflict can be the *protagonist*'s struggle against fate, nature, society, or another person.

FIRST-PERSON POINT OF VIEW

> A literary style in which the *narrator* tells the story from his or her own *point of view* and refers to himself or herself as "I." The narrator may be an active participant in the story or just an observer.

HERO / HEROINE

> The principal *character* in a literary work or *narrative*.

IMAGERY

> Language that brings to mind sense-impressions, representing things that can be seen, smelled, heard, tasted, or touched.

MOTIF

> A recurring idea, structure, contrast, or device that develops or informs the major *themes* of a work of literature.

NARRATIVE

> A story.

LITERARY ANALYSIS

NARRATOR

The person (sometimes a *character*) who tells a story; the *voice* assumed by the writer. The narrator and the author of the work of literature are not the same person.

PLOT

The arrangement of the events in a story, including the sequence in which they are told, the relative emphasis they are given, and the causal connections between events.

POINT OF VIEW

The *perspective* that a *narrative* takes toward the events it describes.

PROTAGONIST

The main *character* around whom the story revolves.

SETTING

The location of a *narrative* in time and space. Setting creates mood or atmosphere.

SUBPLOT

A secondary *plot* that is of less importance to the overall story but may serve as a point of contrast or comparison to the main plot.

SYMBOL

An object, *character*, figure, or color that is used to represent an abstract idea or concept. Unlike an *emblem*, a symbol may have different meanings in different contexts.

SYNTAX

The way the words in a piece of writing are put together to form lines, phrases, or clauses; the basic structure of a piece of writing.

THEME

A fundamental and universal idea explored in a literary work.

TONE

The author's attitude toward the subject or *characters* of a story or poem or toward the reader.

VOICE

An author's individual way of using language to reflect his or her own personality and attitudes. An author communicates voice through *tone, diction*, and *syntax*.

A Note on Plagiarism

Plagiarism—presenting someone else's work as your own—rears its ugly head in many forms. Many students know that copying text without citing it is unacceptable. But some don't realize that even if you're not quoting directly, but instead are paraphrasing or summarizing, *it is plagiarism* unless you cite the source.

Here are the most common forms of plagiarism:

- Using an author's phrases, sentences, or paragraphs without citing the source
- Paraphrasing an author's ideas without citing the source
- Passing off another student's work as your own

How do you steer clear of plagiarism? You should *always* acknowledge all words and ideas that aren't your own by using quotation marks around verbatim text or citations like footnotes and endnotes to note another writer's ideas. For more information on how to give credit when credit is due, ask your teacher for guidance or visit www.sparknotes.com.

REVIEW & RESOURCES

QUIZ

1. What is Wang Lung's reaction upon first seeing O-lan?

   A. He thinks that she is pretty
   B. He thinks she is ugly
   C. He is disappointed that she has bound feet
   D. He is disappointed that she does not have bound feet

2. What does O-lan think of Wang Lung in the early days of their marriage?

   A. She thinks he is cruel because he beats her
   B. She seems pleased with him
   C. She is worried because he spends too much money
   D. She is unhappy because he expects her to do all the work

3. What does *The Good Earth* reveal about the status of women in traditional Chinese culture?

   A. That women are accorded a relatively equal position to men
   B. That women have more power and influence than men have
   C. That women are valued only if they produce many daughters for their husbands
   D. That although there are a variety of roles for women, none of the roles are equal to men's roles

4. Why can't Wang Lung refuse his uncle's demands?

    A. His uncle has helped him in the past, so Wang Lung owes him

    B. Because his uncle has no heirs, Wang Lung hopes to inherit his land and wealth

    C. Traditional Chinese culture dictates young people's obedience to their elders

    D. Wang Lung's father is very close to his brother, and it would anger him if Wang Lung did not give in to his brother's demands

5. Why does Wang Lung rent the House of Hwang?

    A. It satisfies him to move into the house where he was once treated like a lowly serf

    B. He wants to move his uncle's family there so that he can be free of their constant pestering

    C. Lotus complains that his old house isn't good enough for her

    D. All of the above

6. How does Wang Lung deal with the problems his uncle causes him?

    A. He drowns his uncle

    B. He casts his uncle and his uncle's family out of his home

    C. He has Pear Blossom poison his uncle and his uncle's family

    D. He buys opium for his uncle and his uncle's family

7. What does Wang Lung do with O-lan's two pearls?

    A. He sells them to buy opium for his uncle and his uncle's family

    B. He gives them to Lotus

    C. He buys more land with them

    D. He gives them to their second daughter before she is married

8. Why does Wang Lung rise to wealth and influence?

    A. He works hard and manages his money carefully
    B. O-lan works hard and is a resourceful, frugal wife
    C. Luck
    D. All of the above

9. What happens to the second infant daughter born to Wang Lung and O-lan?

    A. O-lan smothers her because she is born during a famine year
    B. O-lan smothers her because she has no interest in having a second daughter
    C. O-lan and Wang Lung sell her as a slave to a rich family
    D. She starves to death

10. Which of the following best characterizes Wang Lung's religion?

    A. Atheism
    B. A combination of Taoism, Buddhism, and earth deity worship
    C. Christianity
    D. Ancestor-worship

11. How does Wang Lung resemble Old Master Hwang?

    A. He loses all respect and attachment to his land
    B. He allows his wife to become hopelessly addicted to opium
    C. He wastes his money by taking a long succession of young concubines
    D. None of the above

12. Judging from *The Good Earth*, what color has special significance in traditional Chinese culture?

    A. Blue
    B. Red
    C. Green
    D. Brown

REVIEW & RESOURCES

13. Why is Wang Lung so devastated by Ching's death?

   A. Ching was Wang Lung's devoted friend and servant for many years
   B. He fears that the loss of Ching as overseer will make his workers less disciplined
   C. Ching was his beloved uncle
   D. None of the above

14. Why is there so much hostility between Wang Lung's two oldest sons?

   A. Wang Lung's older son thinks his younger brother is trying to seduce his wife
   B. Wang Lung's younger son hates his older brother after he finds out that he visits Lotus alone, a shameful and embarrassing breach of filial piety
   C. The older son wants to sell the land, but the younger wishes to keep it
   D. None of the above

15. What happens to Wang Lung's third son?

   A. He becomes an officer in a revolutionary army
   B. He dies in a war
   C. Wang Lung disowns him after he finds out that he is visiting Lotus alone
   D. He starves to death in a famine year

16. What happens to Wang Lung's retarded daughter?

   A. Wang Lung poisons her before he dies
   B. Pear Blossom promises to care for her after Wang Lung's death
   C. O-lan smothers her as soon as it becomes apparent that she is retarded
   D. Wang Lung and O-lan are forced to sell her as a slave during a famine year

17. How does Wang Lung feel about his affair with Pear Blossom?

    A. He feels ashamed because he has committed adultery
    B. He feels guilty because it hurts Lotus's feelings
    C. He feels a little ashamed because he grew up disdaining the decadent behavior of the rich
    D. He feels entitled to the affair because he is the reigning male in his household

18. How do Wang Lung's sons feel about his affair with Pear Blossom?

    A. His oldest son is impressed
    B. His second son does not react
    C. His third son is angry because he asked for Pear Blossom
    D. All of the above

19. Which of the following best describes Wang Lung's relationship with his sons?

    A. It is tense, because they all rebel against his way of life and his plans for them
    B. It is tense, because they show no respect for him at all
    C. It is tender, because they are as devoted to him as Wang Lung is to his own father
    D. None of the above

20. Why does O-lan hate Cuckoo?

    A. Cuckoo is responsible for Wang Lung's decision to buy Lotus as his concubine
    B. Cuckoo has an affair with Wang Lung
    C. Cuckoo's son takes her teenage son to an old prostitute in town
    D. When they were both slaves in the House of Hwang, Cuckoo insulted and abused her

REVIEW & RESOURCES

21. When does Wang Lung come to appreciate everything that O-lan has done for him?

    A. When he takes her pearls and purchases land with them
    B. Right after he moves Lotus into his house
    C. When O-lan becomes bedridden, and the household quickly falls into disorder
    D. Years after her death

22. In *The Good Earth,* what is the only good thing that truly lasts?

    A. Family loyalty
    B. Wealth
    C. Tradition
    D. The land

23. When Wang Lung is ready to get married, why does his father oppose his choice of a pretty woman?

    A. Wang Lung's hard life as a poor farmer will ruin her beauty and it will go to waste
    B. He fears that a pretty wife will always be distracting Wang Lung from his work
    C. He fears that a pretty wife will cause too much jealousy among the other village men
    D. He fears that she is not a virgin

24. Why does Wang Lung send his younger daughter to her future husband's family so early?

    A. Her suitor's mother-in-law is terminally ill, and she is anxious to see her son married before she dies
    B. Wang Lung's uncle has shown an unusual interest in her, so Wang Lung is afraid that he cannot protect her virginity any longer
    C. The son of Wang Lung's uncle has shown an unusual interest in her, so Wang Lung is afraid that he cannot protect her virginity any longer
    D. Wang Lung cannot afford to support her, but her suitor's family can

25. When Lotus comes to Wang Lung's household, what is her primary purpose?

  A. To bear sons for Wang Lung
  B. To help O-lan with the household duties
  C. To satisfy Wang Lung's sexual appetite
  D. All of the above

ANSWER KEY

1: D; 2: B; 3: D; 4: C; 5: A; 6: D; 7: B; 8: D; 9: A; 10: B; 11: D; 12:
B; 13: A; 14: D; 15: A; 16: B; 17: C; 18: D; 19: A; 20: D; 21: C; 22:
D; 23: D; 24: C; 25: C

SUGGESTIONS FOR FURTHER READING

BUCK, PEARL S. *Peony: A Novel of China.* New York: Bloch, 1997.

CONN, PETER J. *Pearl S. Buck: A Cultural Biography.* New York: Cambridge University Press, 1996.

DOYLE, PAUL A. *Pearl S. Buck.* Boston: Twayne Publishers, 1980.

GAO, XIONGYA. *Pearl S. Buck's Chinese Women Characters.* Selinsgrove, Pennsylvania: Susquehanna University Press, 2000.

LEONG, KAREN J. *The China Mystique: Pearl S. Buck, Anna May Wong, Mayling Soon, and the Transformation of American Orientalism.* Berkeley and Los Angeles: University of California Press, 2005.

LEVY, HOWARD S. *The Lotus Lovers: The Complete History of the Curious Erotic Custom of Footbinding in China.* Buffalo, New York: Prometheus Books, 1992.

LIAO, KANG. *Pearl S. Buck: A Cultural Bridge Across the Pacific.* Westport, Connecticut: Greenwood Press, 1997.

LIPSCOLM, ELIZABETH J., FRANCES E. WEBB, and PETER CONN, eds. *The Several Worlds of Pearl S. Buck.* Westport, Connecticut: Greenwood Press, 1994.